CW00810902

A LIBERAL AND GODLY DEAN

The Life of Edward Carpenter

Michael De-la-Noy

'Scholar, Reconciler, Friend'

By the same author

Elgar: The Man

Denton Welch: The Making of a Writer

The Honours System

Acting as Friends: The Story of the Samaritans

Eddy: The Life of Edward Sackville-West

Michael Ramsey: A Portrait

Windsor Castle: Past and Present

Exploring Oxford

The Church of England: A Portrait

The Queen Behind the Throne

The King Who Never Was: The Story of Frederick, Prince of Wales

Mervyn Stockwood: A Lonely Life

Bedford School: A History

The House of Hervey: A History of Tainted Talent

Sutton Pocket Biographies

Scott of the Antarctic

George IV

Edited

The Journals of Denton Welch

The Collected Short Writings of Denton Welch

For Lilian

Obviously

A Liberal and Godly Dean

© 2000 the estate of Michael De-la-Noy, published 2016.

'The Modern Churchman' from *The Deans* by Trevor Beeson,
SCM Press, London 2004, is reproduced by kind permission
of the author and publisher.

Selections from *The Old Boys' Network:*
A Headmaster's Diaries 1972 - 1986
by John Rae, Short Books, London 2009, are reproduced
by kind permission of Daphne Rae and the publisher.

CONTENTS

AUTHOR'S NOTE

I was invited by Edward Carpenter's children, David, Michael, Paul and Louise, to write his biography, and to that extent the book is authorised. But although they, together with Edward's widow Lilian, have gone far beyond the call of duty in the dispersement of help and hospitality they have at no time or in any way attempted to influence what I have written. That they have pointed me in various directions goes without saying, but the confidence they have shown, by placing in my hands the life of a greatly loved and revered husband and father, has been total and not, I hope, abused. There seems no harm in saying at the outset that I believe Edward Carpenter was a great dean, an important scholar and - although this might not necessarily have followed - a great man. He may have made enemies but if he did I have failed to track them down; he exhibited many of the unselfconscious eccentricities of the saintly; and those who automatically look to a biography for scandal, especially, perhaps, in the biography of an Anglican cleric, are going to be disappointed. Edward Carpenter's foibles were of the most human and endearing kind, his integrity, especially in acknowledging profound disappointments, without stain. Whether this made him at all times an entirely compatible husband and father is not for me to say. It does seem, however, that by some amazing juggling act he held together - to an extent all the more extraordinary when one considers his workload, achievements and the hours during which he laboured - his service to the Church, to his family and to the numerous causes in which he passionately believed.

Edward Carpenter was never inactive nor yet too busy to attend to the most humble person or task, and it has been a privilege to attempt to piece together the career of one of the Church of England's most industrious and faithful sons. Inevitably, by its nature, the life of any clergyman is largely ephemeral, but the legacy of remembered kindness and sheer goodness left behind by Carpenter was unusual by any standards. But in his case, much that he achieved at Westminster Abbey has endured, and will continue to do so. When he was appointed a canon residentiary in 1951 Victorian cobwebs still hung in the cloisters. His astonishing 34 years as a member of the Chapter encompassed liturgical experiment, the quickening of a campaign for the ordination of women and ground-breaking advances in the ecumenical movement. He was the most innovative dean of Westminster since Arthur Stanley, dean from 1864 to 1881. Although ructions occurred from time to time, Edward Carpenter created a family atmosphere throughout the precincts, threw open the deanery to one and all, and the Abbey itself to multi-faith services for the

Commonwealth one day, for a service for guide dogs the next. No future dean of Westminster can afford to imitate Edward Carpenter blindly, but no future dean can afford to ignore the pioneering work he did to link the nation's most potent religious shrine with the secular world on its doorstep.

Dean Trevor Beeson has been very generous with his responses to a string of queries, in sparing the time to read and make helpful comments on the manuscript, and in granting permission for extensive quotations to be made from a volume of his diaries, *Window on Westminster*. And in addition to Edward Carpenter's immediate family I am grateful to the following for their help and cooperation: Mr Jeremy Bagwell Purefoy of the Central Chancery of the Orders of Knighthood; the Rt Rev John Baker; Canon William Barnard; the Rev Marcus Braybrooke; Miss Joanna Brendon; the Very Rev Tony Bridge; Dr Alexandrina Buchanan, assistant archivist at Lambeth Palace Library; Major General David Burden, Receiver General of Westminster Abbey; Fr David Campbell, SSJE; the Very Reverend Wesley Carr, Dean of Westminster; Mrs Samantha Chandler; the Rev Oswold Clarke; Mr Harry Coles; Professor Frank Cox; Sir Hugh Cubitt; Mrs Elma Dangerfield; Mr Nadir Dinshaw; Miss Sarah Dodgson, Librarian at the Athenaeum; Mr Clive Edwards of the SCM-Canterbury Press; Mr Geoffrey Fallows; the Rev Tim Gosden; the Rev Janet Grierson, Miss Millicant Harris; the Rev Anthony Harvey; Lady Felicity Harwood; the Rev Nicholas Henderson, general secretary of the Modern Churchpeoples' Union; Miss Viola Huggins; the Rev Gerard Irvine; Canon Eric James; the Rev Roger Job; Mr Tristram Jones-Parry, Head Master of Westminster School; Mr Michael Keall; the Rt Rev Edward Knapp-Fisher; the Rev Robert Lee; the Rev Andrew Linzey; Canon Alan Luff; Dame Jean Maxwell-Scott; the Very Rev Michael Mayne; the Rev J Fraser McLuskey; Mrs Susan Mold, Librarian at Strode's College; the Rt Rev Hugh Montefiore; Mr Andrew Morris; Dr Richard Mortimer, Keeper of the Muniments at Westminster Abbey; Mr Robert Newell; Dr Richard Palmer, Librarian at Lambeth Palace; Canon Jim Richardson; Mrs Frances Hodges Roper; the late Rt Rev Lord Runcie; Lady Sandford; Mr Bryan Saunders; Canon Eric Saxon; the Rt Rev David Say; Miss Elizabeth Selby, archives assistant at King's College, London; Mr E A Smith, archivist at Westminster School; Mrs Jeremy Thorpe; Mrs Shirley Trefusis; Dr Tony Trowles, librarian at Westminster Abbey; Mrs Gladys Whittaker; and Miss Catherine Wilson.

LIST OF PLATES

1. Edward Carpenter and Lilian Wright at the time of their engagement

2. The Mothers' Union Coach Party at Stanmore c. 1946 – Edward far left and Lilian front row far left

3. Lilian and Edward outside the Rectory at Stanmore with Edward's brother, Harry, his parents and David as a baby in 1947

4. Edward's parents, Fred and Kate Carpenter, at Brighton in 1946

5. Official photograph of Edward when he was appointed a Canon of Westminster in 1951

6. The Queen being introduced to the new Canon by Dean Alan Don c. 1951

7. The Carpenter family on Leith Hill, Surrey, in 1961

8. The Carpenter family gathered in the garden of No 5 Little Cloister, on the occasion of Edward's Installation as Dean of Westminster, May 1974

9. Mr Dean on his bicycle in Parliment Square

10. Celebrating His Holiness, The Dalai Lama's 49th birthday in the Deanery Drawing Room in 1984

11. Lilian and Edward in the garden of their home in Richmond c. 1996

MAJOR CHRONOLOGY

1910 27 November born New Haw, Surrey.

1915 St Paul's Boys' School, Addlestone.

1922 Strode's Secondary School for Boys, Egham.

1929 King's College, London.

1932 First Class Honours degree in History.

  Gladstone Memorial History Prize.

  Barry Prize for Divinity.

1933 Entered Faculty of Theology, King's College.

1934 MA in History with Distinction.

1935 BD and AKC with a First.

  Ordained deacon and appointed assistant curate,

  Holy Trinity, Marylebone, London

1936 Ordained priest

  Thomas Sherlock

1941 Assistant curate, St Mary's, Harrow-on-the-Hill, Middlesex

  Married Lilian Betsy Wright, Holy Trinity, Marylebone

1943 PhD

1945 Rector St John the Evangelist, Great Stanmore, Middlesex

1946 24 December birth of eldest son, David

1949 11 April birth of second son, Michael

  Thomas Tenison: His Life and Times

1951 Canon Residentiary, Westminster Abbey

1953 *That Man Paul*

     7 June birth of youngest son, Paul

1954 Fellow of King's College, London

     The Nineteenth Century Country Parson with A Tindal Hart

1956 *The Protestant Bishop*

1957 Contributor to *A History of St Paul's Cathedral*

1958 Lector Theologiae

1959 Treasurer

1960 28 July birth of daughter, Louise

1961 *Common Sense About Christian Ethics*

1963 Archdeacon of Westminster

     The Church's Use of the Bible

1965 *The Service of a Parson*

1966 Edits and contributes to *A House of Kings: The Official History of Westminster Abbey*

1971 *Cantuar: The Archbishops in their Office*

1974 Dean of Westminster

1976 Contributor to *Man of Christian Action*

1985 Retires

     KCVO

1987 *Westminster Abbey*, illustrated by David Gentleman

1991 *Archbishop Fisher: His Life and Times*

1998 26 August dies Twickenham, Middlesex

     4 September Funeral, Westminster Abbey

The author

Michael De-la-Noy was educated at Bedford School, whose history he wrote in 1999. From 1962-65 he was Religious Editor of Prism Publications and from 1967-70 he served as press officer to the archbishop of Canterbury, Michael Ramsey, whose biography, *Michael Ramsey: A Portrait*, he published in 1990. In 1993 he wrote *The Church of England: A Portrait*, described by one reviewer as 'prose with personality', and three years later, to critical acclaim, he published a biography of Mervyn Stockwood, the controversial bishop of Southwark. His other biographies include lives of Elgar, Denton Welch, Edward Sackville-West, Frederick, Prince of Wales and Queen Elizabeth the Queen Mother, which became a bestseller in 1994. He has also written histories of the Honours System, the Samaritans, Windsor Castle and the Hervey family. He was a contributor to both the Missing Persons volume of the *Dictionary of National Biography* and the *New Dictionary of National Biography*. In *Who's Who* he described his recreation as 'going for very short walks.'

Michael De-la-Noy died in 2002 leaving the manuscript of this biography of Edward Carpenter, which was written in 2000, unpublished. Edward's family have subsequently edited the text, principally to correct factual errors. They have not updated the text and it has not been possible to complete or update the footnotes. They have added an appendix which complements De-la-Noy's text.

One

CRAFTSMEN AND BUILDERS

Edward Frederick Carpenter was born on 27 November 1910 in the front bedroom of No 17 New Haw Road, Addlestone, in Surrey, just 23 miles from London. It was in or very near London that he was to spend the whole of his 50 years in the ordained ministry, an astonishing 34 of them at Westminster Abbey. But his family roots were firmly planted in the countryside, and although a metropolitan environment became essential to him as far as work, both clerical and academic, was concerned, it was to the tranquillity of the west country, to places like Tiverton and Washfield in Devon, that he would always turn a wistful eye. That he seldom spoke about his childhood - and when he did he appeared to do so with no great interest or enthusiasm - may perhaps indicate that it was a contented one. He certainly retained all his life a deep affection for his parents and feelings of gratitude towards them.

Edward was the younger son of Frederick James Carpenter and Jessie Kate Arscott, and through his father he inherited some unexpected but surely beneficial Jewish blood, accounting perhaps to some extent for his Judaistic enjoyment of family life and his sympathy for those marginalized by society, not to mention his association with the London Society of Jews and Christians. However, Edward's paternal grandmother, the source of his Jewish inheritance, has been described as a cantankerous woman, and quite apart from the fact that Edward's grandfather, Henry James Carpenter, was a devout Anglican, it has always remained a mystery how he and Elizabeth Jacobs ever came to marry. Henry, born in 1851, was a master craftsman and builder whose forbears had moved from Norwich - from the centre of another exclusively rural part of England - to settle at Little Keyford, on the outskirts of Frome in Somerset, 15 miles to the south of Bath and close enough to the border of Wiltshire for him to be summoned by the marquess of Bath to carry out repairs at Longleat House. There are however no records at Longleat of Henry being employed there. Neither does there seem to be any proof of another alleged family connection with Longleat, the birth to a Carpenter girl in service at the house of an illegitimate child fathered by a younger son. She is even said to have been given a cottage on the estate (an uncommonly generous act on the part of wayward aristocracy if true) and to have adopted the Bath family name, Thynn, pronounced Thin and sometimes spelt Thynne. As this event apparently took place early in the eighteenth century the girl, even if her name was Carpenter, may not necessarily have been connected with Edward's family.

Edward's vocation to the priesthood can in no way be attributed to his grandfather's example of religious observance - Henry died three years before Edward was born - but in 1907 it was recorded by the local newspaper that Henry Carpenter was a lifelong member of the congregation of Christ Church, Frome, and that 'his churchmanship was of a solid and consistent stamp.' He taught in the Sunday School for 38 years, under the supervision of no fewer than three incumbents and 20 assistant curates, and he left his mark in a number of country churches restored by the firm for which he worked, Messrs Brown, later Messrs Grant Bros. 'Though quiet and unobtrusive' Henry's life had been 'eminently useful', and as well as teaching for so many years in the Sunday School he acted as a sidesman and a member of the Church Council. Unlike his grandson (Edward's politics leaned to the left) he had apparently always been a 'staunch Conservative', and on the day of his death the Frome Conservative Club's flag was flown at half-mast.

Henry was only 56 when he died - from a haemorrhage, according to the parish magazine, after 'a long and trying illness' if the local newspaper is to be believed, but possibly a haemorrhage was the final and fatal outcome of the long illness. Henry's daughter, Edward Carpenter's Aunt Emily, was also destined to endure 'months of suffering, borne with true Christian fortitude and cheerfulness.' Like many spinsters who themselves eschew marriage and the chance of having children of their own, Emily was drawn to teaching by a genuine love of other people, and she became senior assistant mistress at Christ Church Girls' School in Frome. In 1914 she was appointed headmistress of Minehead Girls' School, and in 1920 she was admitted as a member of the Royal Society of Teachers. Obviously of a kindly disposition, Emily Carpenter thought nothing of nipping to the chemist to buy cough mixture for an ailing pupil, and always kept a supply of dry clothes for girls to change into when they were caught in the rain. In Minehead she worked as a volunteer to help those with tuberculosis, in her day still a particular scourge of the young. And although, like her father, she was a devout Anglican, Emily did not hesitate to direct girls of another allegiance to their respective pastor or minister, and her sense of ecumenical propriety found an echo in her nephew's later career.

Edward used to stay at Minehead with his aunt, and was 19 when he saw her on her deathbed in 1930. She was dying of cancer, and her last request was for strawberries and cream. She had suffered, in a fairly mild manner, from the perverse nature of her cantankerous mother, who preferred boys to girls, not an uncommon trait among Jewish mothers; apparently whenever Emily brought her fellow schoolteachers to tea cracked teacups would be produced, the best china being preserved for a visit from the chimneysweep. Elizabeth Carpenter's most serious crime however was the destruction on Henry's death of all his papers, including, it is said, a history of the Carpenter family.

It had only been a matter of weeks prior to Henry's death that in December 1906 his younger son Frederick James, the father of Edward, married Jessie Kate Arscott at St Mary the Virgin, Washfield, a Devon village two and a half miles to the north-west of Tiverton. A local reporter observed it was a pretty wedding, and that 'the bells were merrily rung during the afternoon'. Three generations of bellringers would have been responsible for the peels, ranging from 11-year-old Ernest Bowden, whose ancestor Robert Bowden had been churchwarden in 1576, to Isaac Snell, aged 78, who went on ringing the bells until he was 90. And it must indeed have been a lovely setting, the present church dating mainly from the fifteenth century and boasting a fine Jacobean screen, and over it a royal coat of arms dated 1624. Like Henry Carpenter, Kate's father, Thomas Arscott, 'a very gentle man', was an esteemed Washfield craftsman, but also a wheelwright, carpenter, 'Plain House Painter' and 'Sash Glazier' who advertised 'general repairs in Building at moderate charges.' From 1907 to 1924 he served as churchwarden at Washfield. The unusual name Arscott has been claimed for north Devon but it may possibly be a mixture of English and Cornish. From 1530 to 1537 a John Arscott was rector of Holsworthy in north Devon, but by the turn of the twentieth century Arscott had nearly died out as a surname, more commonly being used as a Christian name.

Thomas Arscott, Edward's maternal grandfather, was born in 1854 at South Tawton in Devon, just to the east of Okehampton, but early in life he settled at Washfield, earning his living as a builder. It was at Washfield that Thomas met Edward's grandmother, Ellen, who had been born at Cornwood on the edge of Dartmoor, a few miles east of Plymouth. She moved to Washfield in 1883, to work as a nanny for a rather grand family called de Las Casas, when she and Thomas were both aged 30. They lived at the end of a terrace of houses oddly called The Weeches, and Ellen, 'of a very happy and sympathetic disposition', was said to enter with her husband wholeheartedly into everything taking place in the village. She died on 8 January 1933, her funeral at Washfield not, it seems, being attended by Edward, although a wreath arrived 'To dear

Grandma from her loving grandchildren and great-grandchildren.' After his wife's death Thomas decided to retire, and put up for sale by auction much of his stock-in-trade and furniture. These included seven ladders 'varying from 7 rungs to 18', two carpenter's benches, an 'old pram', a 'half tester mahogany bedstead with curtains', a feather bed, a 'large meat safe' and a coal scuttle. Having sold up he left Washfield to live with one of his daughters at Burlescombe, not far from Tiverton, 'where his genial nature again caused him to be greatly beloved by all who had the privilege to know him.' Thomas survived Ellen by a decade, dying in 1943. The story goes that, winding up his watch and with a daughter on each side, he recited the Lord's Prayer and the Nunc Dimittis and then died peacefully in his chair. His body was brought back to Washfield to lie beside his wife, being committed to the ground by his grandson Edward, by this time an assistant curate at Holy Trinity, Marylebone. A personal appreciation in the local newspaper asserted that Thomas Arscott's happy home life had been the kind 'that has helped to make England what she is today.'

The concept of creating a happy home certainly seems to have rubbed off on to his son-in-law, Frederick James, the father of Edward, born in 1880, late enough to imbue his sons with old-fashioned Victorian virtues. Frederick was 27 when his first boy, Henry, was born, in 1907. Henry, known as Harry, went into banking, and by the time of his marriage in 1937 he had for 13 years been on the staff of Barclays Bank in Woking. Soon after their marriage, Frederick James and his wife had deserted the West Country for suburban Surrey and so Henry was baptised on 19 January 1908 at Cobham and Edward on New Year's Day 1911 at Addlestone. Hence Edward was able to record with certainty the first fact about his life - that he had been born in Addlestone. To the north, the house still looked on to open fields, and when quite late in life Edward made a half-hearted shot at drafting an autobiography he recalled that thanks to the open land, an eighteenth century farmhouse still provided 'a picturesque reminder of the great Age of Reason.' (He told his family that his earliest recollection was of being carried on the shoulders of a German prisoner of war billeted at the farm.) So drawn was Edward to the Age of Reason that one of his literary heroes - perhaps the character from history he loved most - was Shelley, and it was after scribbling a mere four pages of manuscript about himself that Edward easily got side-tracked, feeling irresistibly compelled to start writing about the tragic poet. Percy Bysshe Shelley, sent down from University College, Oxford for being an atheist and drowned at the age of 29, appealed both to the Romantic in Edward and to his intellectual sympathy for the born outsider.[1]

He does tell us however that on a fine day he could make out - or imagine he could - the spire of Weybridge parish church, a nineteenth century consequence of the Oxford Movement. Also mid-19th century were the 'fifty odd houses built piece meal' at New Haw, a hamlet that lay between Addlestone and Weybridge, 'which so far as we children were concerned constituted our world.' By 'we children' he could only have meant he and his elder brother, and it sounds as if very little travel was involved in Edward's earliest years. He was sent to St Paul's Boys' School in Addlestone (the exact date is unknown but presumably when he was about five or six), and in 1922, at the age of eleven, he came first in a class of 33 boys; it was a very respectable foretaste of a brilliant academic career to come. Out of a possible 228 marks he obtained 167, scoring 18 out of 20 for conduct. One wonders what misdemeanour accounted for the two dropped points. It may have been the occasion when he was caned for talking, and his widow Lilian recalls, 'He never got over the disgrace!' Edward obtained a more surprising 16 out of 20 for handwriting - surprising because as an adult his handwriting was atrocious. On 13 April 1921, and again on 3 March 1922, Edward passed 'a specially satisfactory examination in Religious Knowledge', receiving a certificate to prove it, duly signed by the bishop of Winchester, Edward Talbot. It was Talbot who confirmed Edward, in 1922, presumably confident about laying hands on a boy of only eleven.

From his local school Edward gained a scholarship to Strode's Secondary School in Egham. It became quite obvious that academically Edward was going to outshine his elder brother who attended Woking Grammar School. In the General School Certificate Edward gained credits in English, modern history, geography, arithmetic, elementary mathematics and drawing. By the time he had set his heart on entering London University he had moved on to a distinction in modern history, and gained credits in English, French and mathematics. He won a Surrey County Major university scholarship worth £60 a year for three years, and the school awarded him a leaving exhibition to the same value. Clearly they had faith in his future, for £180 towards a student's expenses in 1928 was not to be sneezed at.

Strode's had been endowed in 1704 by a local businessman, Henry Strode. In 1975 it became a sixth form college. Two salient factors stand out from Edward's achievements as a schoolboy at Strode's: his early and consistent interest in Religious Knowledge and his equal enthusiasm both for work and games. In July 1925 the Second Annual Athletic Sports were held, 'in spite of the fact that the rain was pouring down in torrents for the greater part of the afternoon.' Aged 12, Edward emerged from these damp conditions as winner of the junior half-mile. At the same age he was awarded a special prize for Religious Knowledge. A year later he came out first in his form, and he captured a second prize for Religious Knowledge in December 1924 and again the next year, when he was also - yet again - the winner of a prize for coming first in his form. Soccer was to become a passion, and the school magazine, the *Strodian*, recorded, when Edward had just turned 15, that he had 'played consistently.' As both a batsman and a bowler he seems to have been a more than competent cricketer too. In the summer of 1926 he was named as being among the 'outstanding batsmen' and the 'steadiest bowlers' although unfortunately in a match against the Old Boys he managed to get himself run out for 10.

Christmas of that year saw Edward awarded yet another prize for Religious Knowledge. At soccer he got promoted to the 1st XI, and it was reported that playing at right-half he was, perhaps, 'the most outstanding player in the team, owing to the way in which he overcomes his disadvantages in height and weight, for he is a match for all the opposing forwards that we meet, and strengthens the defence enormously.' With such skills on the football field and cricket pitch it is hard to imagine he was other than a popular boy. In the summer of 1927, when he was 16, he was awarded his 1st XI colours, and was elected to the cricket committee. By the start of the Christmas term 1927 he had been made a school prefect, initially on probation; his status as a prefect was confirmed at half-term. He now also joined the Football Club committee - good training for any future cleric, for whom committee work can consume all too much valuable time.

Where soccer was concerned that term we learn, if somewhat ungrammatically, that 'Our chief weaknesses were in the inside positions, but the removal of Carpenter from the half-back line to the inside-left berth has done much to remedy the problem. Carpenter makes up for his lack of weight by his ability to secure the ball, of which (sic) he usefully disposes.' By this time Edward had graduated to the Sixth Form, in which he matriculated with a distinction in History. The following summer, of 1928, Edward featured among those boys who had 'bowled well all through the season' and had 'captured most opponents' wickets at low cost.' In his last year he gained his Higher School Certificate, and by now he was the second most senior prefect.

Before Edward had exhausted his childhood memories in favour of a dissertation on Shelley he recalled the Black Horse public house, 200 yards away, where 'my spendthrift but lovable Uncle Frank spent much of his time.' Edgar Frank Carpenter was the eldest son of Henry James Carpenter. He had been born at Frome in 1878, became a carpenter and joiner, and although he died at the age of 80 in Addlestone he was buried at Christ Church, Frome, one of those conducting his service being his nephew, by now a canon of Westminster. Other, more prosaic, recollections included flying kites and playing football in the street, but there was one 'sport', as Edward designated it, in which he indulged which he recalled 'bitterly and with shame and contrition', fishing. Once Edward discovered that Shelley had been a vegetarian he became one too - as did his wife and three of his four children.

It seems that at Strode's there was a master whose Christian faith had been shattered by his experience of the Great War. Edward wrote: 'For some reason or other - I never knew why - the school authorities decided to transfer him from teaching Latin to English literature. The result was that he now discovered a Faith, an inspiration and a challenge in the works of Shelley. I myself caught the contagion of his enthusiasm, and Shelley, throughout my life, has remained a uniquely compelling influence.' (Edward's widow, Lilian Carpenter, believes there was 'a lot of Shelley in Edward, who was very stoical with great physical energy.') Unusual, not to say eccentric, schoolmasters were two-a-penny in Edward's time. His art master was apparently in the habit of marking his pupils' paintings not in line with their artistic merits but according to the boys' behaviour .

Edward's father, an 'outgoing man with a great sense of humour' according to his daughter-in-law, must have gazed with some astonishment on his younger son's achievements thus far, for he himself had been compelled to leave school at the age of 12. Unlike his own father, Frederick James Carpenter, although he voted Liberal in 1906 (something he regretted), when he was 26, was 'a great Labour man', and it is reasonable to assume his father's political persuasions had some influence, for Edward's instincts and sympathies were always to the left of centre. One parental example that failed to catch on was his mother's almost obsessive tidiness. It is possible that her very tidiness contributed to Edward's untidyness. She did everything for him. Few sporty or academic boys - and Edward was both - take kindly to being told to sort out the mess in their bedroom. But everything in Edward's childhood home was expected to be in its right place; everything was very orderly; no weeds were permitted in the garden. In adult life Edward would not have distinguished between bindweed and the passion flower it was strangling, and lack of interest in sartorial elegance meant that bicycle clips remained in place indoors and vestments might be flung on any old how. But Kate's house-trained nature came naturally to her; in the households in which she had worked as a nursemaid and governess not a speck of dust would have been permitted to lie undisturbed for a split second. She was a good cook, which unfortunately was another attribute somewhat lost on Edward, who had virtually no interest in culinary delights whatsoever. What Kate gave Edward most crucially was unconditional love. Edward's eventual fiancée warned both mother and son that she would never be able to love

Edward as much as Kate had done, and Edward returned his mother's affection in full. They were devoted to one another.

That bond must surely have been formed when it appeared, soon after Edward's birth, that he might never be able to see. As a very small baby he was in and out of Moorfields Eye Hospital, had to be protected from electric lights, and from earliest childhood always wore spectacles. But the handicap of poor eyesight never proved a bar to learning; he read assiduously as a boy, developing in such a way as to prompt a former canon of Westminster and bishop of Salisbury, John Baker, to comment after his death, 'He was someone of the widest intellectual reading and interests that I have ever known.'[2] It was in his skill at games too that Edward demonstrated a remarkable ability to master poor eyesight; his prowess at tennis was such that many people believed he could have played as a professional. Edward himself always considered that he could have been both a professional footballer and cricketer – especially a cricketer as a slow bowler. An interesting trait of developing intellectualism displayed at school was his preference for the company of boys older than himself; he simply reasoned that their conversation would be more interesting than that of his contemporaries or juniors. Conversation, along with walking and Association Football (Chelsea was the club he supported), was listed among his recreations in *Who's Who*. 'The Dean won't be into Evensong tonight' the Westminster Abbey choir boys would say if Chelsea was playing at home.

Edward's love for his mother was by no means exclusive; he revered his father, a man, as his obituary put it when he died in 1969 at the age of 90, 'of remarkable vitality and intellectual ability and vision', who could 'hold a conversation on many subjects.' It seems that Frederick Carpenter 'created for himself a legion of friends who admired not only his ability but his farsightedness, tolerance and warmth of character.' Determined that others should benefit from the formal education he never received, he served as a member of the local schools' board and was a School Manager at Addlestone for 46 years.

In following a strong family tradition of craftsmanship and worship, Frederick Carpenter supervised the building of the chancel and vestry of St Paul's Church, Addlestone, having established his own building firm. Up in the Addlestone area went detached, semi-detached and terraced houses, all of them, so his grandson David Carpenter recalls, 'in that ubiquitous 1930's pebble-dash style.'[3] It was in one of his own houses in Addlestone Park, which they called 'Velvines', that Frederick and Kate settled after moving from New Haw Road to Conquest Road. It was detached and 'looked larger than it was', although there were in fact four bedrooms; there was also a garage in which was housed a Rover car, purchased in 1949, and about half an acre of garden. From some of his properties Frederick collected rent, thinking it more prudent to do so on a bicycle rather than in the Rover. And there was little likelihood of him being mugged; protected tenancy laws kept the value of rented properties very low. Edward's parents would not have been described as wealthy but comfortably off. David Carpenter has written of his grandfather, 'He believed very much in fair dealing, honesty and high standards of workmanship. His craft/Christian background gave him an independence and self-confidence. He was a hardy, high-principled, hard-working impressive man.

'I remember staying with him around 1960 [when David would have been about 14] during the winter and being absolutely freezing in the house. As a great concession he allowed me to open one door of a stove, but thought I was very pathetic asking for it.'

Self-reliance, confidence, total honesty; these were some of the qualities Edward undoubtedly inherited or acquired from his father. Edward once cycled miles back to a village shop because he thought he had inadvertently short-changed them. When he went through customs 'he would compile elaborate lists of everything we had bought.' Frederick Carpenter was also someone confident in his own values. He was no respecter of persons simply because of rank or status. After his marriage, he worked for his father-in-law, Thomas Arscott, at Washfield. When the local squire failed to pay a bill, Fred went and complained. It was after this incident that an alarmed Thomas Arscott told Fred that perhaps Washfield was not the right place for him. This no doubt precipitated the move to Surrey. Edward inherited this same confidence in himself which meant that, despite the high circles in which he eventually moved, he became neither a snob nor an inverted snob. He was secure in himself and treated everyone the same.

Some time after his wife had died Frederick Carpenter was knocked down by a car. David took his father to the hospital where they found Edward's father 'disorientated and talking nonsense. Coming back in the old Rover I was driving along the side of Hampton Court Park and listening to *Round the Horn* when I suddenly realised that Daddy (who for some reason was sitting in the back) was crying.' By the time Frederick died, in 1969, his younger son was archdeacon of Westminster, and took his funeral service at St Paul's, Addlestone. Lilian Carpenter says that people always left Edward's funerals 'strengthened and uplifted.'

At the time of Edward Carpenter's birth, four years before the outbreak of the Great War, the class system in England was both rigid and far more stratified than it was to become after the war. People knew 'their place in society', whether they were working class, upper working class, lower middle, middle, upper middle or upper class, and it is not in the least surprising to find Edward's mother working as a nanny at the turn of the century; the census of 1841 found almost one in 16 of the population in domestic service. Skilled craftsmen like the Carpenters were not so easy to place, especially if they were self-employed. Coming from a comfortable but not opulent background, Edward's horizons were also shaped by his lack of interest in material things. Perhaps his bad eyesight was also a factor here. Like many truly good and holy people he was not in the least interested in or moved by his environment; a desk was for writing at, it had no need to be eighteenth century and worth £800.

Edward left Strode's at the end of the summer term of 1929, having 'pursued a Course of Higher Study' from September 1926 until July 1929, as a result of which, in 1928, he was awarded a University of London Higher School Certificate in English, modern history and French. In his final term he passed in Latin, English, French and modern history, gaining, for modern history, a Distinction. The fact that Edward's Certificate incorporated the information that the Board of Education had inspected Strode's and 'recognised it as an efficient Secondary School' was to cut no ice with sniffy ecclesiastical colleagues when 22 years later he was appointed to the Chapter of Westminster Abbey without either an Oxbridge degree or a public school education. Edward did in fact think of applying to Cambridge, but said he did not wish to wait a year before starting at University.

Edward merely had a normal summer break before, in its centenary year, he entered King's College, London in October 1929. Three years later he graduated with a First Class Honours degree in history, one of only two students in the College's History Department to gain a First and one of just half a dozen history Firsts in the whole of the University. On completion of his degree he was awarded a History Bursary worth £50, but there was a slight catch; according to a letter from the Principal in Edward's file he was required to give 'some assistance' in the Department. Of far greater distinction was his award of two prestigious prizes, the Barry Prize for Divinity and the Gladstone Memorial History Prize.

By this time Edward had obviously decided on ordination, or at any rate on an academic career in the field of theology, for on 1 July 1933 he applied for admission to the Faculty of Theology, asking if he could commence his course in October that year. It was a firm rule of the Faculty that 'All Candidates must produce a Certificate of good moral and religious character from a Clergyman of their Parish, or of the Parish in which they have last resided.' Edward applied to the vicar of Addlestone, the Reverend H E Peterson, who obliged with the following minimalist testimonial:

I have known Mr Edward Frederick Carpenter from April 1930, when I first came to the parish. He was serving then as a Sunday School Teacher, and has continued to serve in that capacity ever since. I can with my every confidence state that I believe him to be of good moral and religious character.

For further references Edward got in touch with a former schoolteacher, and with 'Mrs R Hadden', who lived at Hazel Hatch, Addlestone. He could have studied for an Associate of King's College course or for a bachelorship of divinity, but decided to go for his AKC and BD qualifications in one combined course. In 1934 he asked to reside at the College Hostel in Vincent Square, realising presumably how heavy his workload was now to become, for he was determined also to study for a History MA, awarded to him in that year with Distinction. The Church historian was up and away. Edward's subject for examination was the 'Religious and Philosophical Background of English Church History from 1702 to 1760,' and for his MA thesis he chose 'his worth for Church and State' of a somewhat obscure but rather remarkable eighteenth century divine, Thomas Sherlock, bishop of Bangor, Salisbury and London; remarkable because he was the only bishop so far to have declined the archbishoprics both of York and Canterbury. Edward's study of Sherlock became his first publication, in 1936, the year of his ordination to the priesthood.

He was still only 25. And those parishioners too busy scraping a living to be much preoccupied with historical or academic matters probably never realised that *Thomas Sherlock*[4] had appeared on the bookstalls. Even the better educated in the parish might have found it rather a tough read. *Thomas Sherlock* will always remain a valuable contribution to eighteenth century ecclesiastical and political history (the two were interwoven) but it was never aimed at the general reader. 'It now remains for the biographer to state a few little personal details about the man himself which have found no place in the former pages' was a sentence, appearing as it did on page 324, that would not have endeared Edward to a modern publisher's editor, and the solidly respectable academic tradition in which he had so recently been trained permeates the whole book. Lord Hervey of Ickworth, for example, that crucial chronicler of the reign of George II and a bosom pal of Queen Caroline, who virtually ran the Church of England from 1727 until her death in 1737, is plopped into the narrative with scarcely a word of explanation as to who he is; Edward must simply have assumed that as his examiners would know of Lord Hervey there was no need to elucidate. Easy as it is to be critical of such a stance at this distance in time, Edward's approach, for better or

worse, was a hallmark of the born academic. What was remarkable about
Edward's personality was the way in which he learned as a pastor to lay
aside his learning, invariably tailoring his own interests to those of the
people he met.

Two

IN THE STEPS OF BYRON

In 1935 Edward Carpenter passed his examination for bachelor of divinity and his AKC with a First. On 24 September that year the head of the Theology Faculty at London University was writing to the Bishop of London, the aged and irrepressible Arthur Winnington-Ingram, now in his 34th year as diocesan, to say that intellectually Edward was 'a very strong candidate [for ordination].' He went on to report that 'During his two years in the Theology Faculty he proved an entirely satisfactory student.' His conduct had always been irreproachable 'and he was a steady, industrious worker.' This amazingly lukewarm letter ended, 'I have no hesitation in recommending him to Your Lordship's favourable consideration, as a suitable candidate for ordination.'

King's College would have concentrated on academic work exclusively. No one would have taken Edward aside and explained how to celebrate Holy Communion, preach a sermon, hear confession, conduct a funeral, trudge round a parish house-visiting; before the Second World War it was simply assumed that a young cleric would be trained by his parish priest, learning the ropes on the job. Hence at the age of 24, one year older than the minimum age permitted by canon law, Edward Carpenter knelt before his father-in-God Arthur Winnington-Ingram in St Paul's Cathedral, to be ordained deacon.

Edward's priesting followed virtually automatically a year later. For a parish in which Edward was to serve his title - his first assistant curacy - Winnington-Ingram chose Holy Trinity, Marylebone. Holy Trinity was in the assured hands of one of the bishop's examining chaplains, George Saywell. It had wealthy parishioners living in the area of Harley Street, a churchwarden, Sir Alfred Wood, who hailed from Hindhead and extremely poor parishioners on the other side of Great Portland Street. The Rector lived at 6 Albany Terrace (he later moved to 8 Hallam Street, and then to No 84), from whence he had written to Edward on 9 July 1935 to say, 'I understand ... that you are contemplating ordination in September & that you are not yet definitely fixed up. I am seeking a man to help me here & I wondered whether you would care to come and see me. This might be the sort of parish you would like to begin work in. We have most of Harley St and the doctors' area in the parish, and a fairly large poor population too, and we have all the usual parochial organisations. You would probably find a good deal of scope here, and interest too.

'The church is of the moderate type, & my own outlook definitely "liberal" - if labels must be used. [Saywell, with a Double First in oriental languages, was a scholarly and cultivated man and an outstanding leader of the Liberal Evangelical Movement.]

'Of course we could neither of us commit ourselves until we have met, and I should be glad to arrange a talk with you if you would care to come & see me.'

Although the London postal service was incredibly expeditious at this time, it is unlikely Edward received this letter before the following day, 10 July, and he evidently telephoned for an appointment and met Saywell within 48 hours, leaving him undecided about his suitability (he may have thought him over-qualified), for the Rector was writing again on the 12th to say, 'I feel that before deciding this very important question we ought perhaps to meet again & have a little more talk. Could you come again tomorrow (Sat), arriving here about 12 & staying for lunch? I shall be engaged after lunch but we could talk beforehand. I shall wish to meet the expenses of your journeys.'

Edward's lunch and second talk failed to clinch the matter. On 14 July the indecisive Mr Saywell was writing again, to say: 'I am afraid I cannot yet be as definite as I had hoped. For many reasons I should like to ask you straight away to come here, but my present lack of a senior curate & your own inexperience in certain directions (about which you spoke to me so frankly yesterday), make me feel that I ought not to decide for a little longer - say a week or more, & in the meantime I can explore the possibilities of securing a senior man temporarily if not permanently. I hope you will forgive my seeming indecision, but the matter is of such importance to me as for yourself.'

What Saywell was obviously trying to balance were Edward's academic qualifications, which for someone seeking his first curacy were pretty astonishing, with his obvious lack - total, in fact - of pastoral experience; the fact that Edward was prepared patiently to hang around may indicate that he believed the parish was right for him.

'Would you then give me another week,' George Saywell pleaded, 'or perhaps a little longer? Of course if you wish to go on seeking a title you must feel free to do so, though I hope you would not accept another without letting me know before your decision is made. I can see it is very important that you should begin in a parish where your special gifts would find full scope.'

By 3 August Saywell, an experienced parish priest of 55 who had been at Holy Trinity since 1925, had at last made up his mind. 'I am writing now to ask you definitely to come to Holy Trinity,' he told Edward that day. 'I am not sure that I mentioned the fact that the stipend at the start is £200 a year. You will need to write to the Bishop of London's chaplain - if you decide to come - to inform him of my offer of a title, & to ask to be allowed to sit for the ordination exam for the Michaelmas ordination. When I hear from you I shall write to the Bishop myself too.

'I am just off for a 13 day cruise so shall not be able to do anything more until I return ... I am sure you will find Holy Trinity a happy sphere if you decide to come, & I am hoping that I shall also have the help of a senior man - which is what has been rather holding me up.

'Trusting that you may be guided in the right direction...'

Until now, Saywell had addressed his potential assistant curate as Dear Mr Carpenter. Once Edward had accepted the offer of a £4 a week curacy (no wonder Saywell was too embarrassed to mention the meagre stipend in conversation, a rate of pay, even allowing for free accommodation which would only have been worth a few shillings a week, that placed Edward in 1935 on pretty well the lowest rung of the economic ladder) he became 'Dear Carpenter.' He was informed, on 21 August, in a letter from St Cloud Hotel, Brockenhurst, that forms had been duly filled in, and that his future Rector had very much enjoyed his cruise. 'The weather was almost perfect, & my visit to Pompeii and Vesuvius was an unforgettable experience.' He hoped Edward too was getting 'some real holiday' before his ordination, and it was not long before Saywell was telling a young Cambridge undergraduate, David Say, consecrated bishop of Rochester in 1960, that if he agreed to half of Edward's suggestions 'the parish would be in a very excited state!'[1]

Like many Anglican churches before the second world war, Holy Trinity teamed with worthy organisations: Scouts, Guides, Mothers' Meetings, Knitting Parties all had their activities recorded in the parish magazine (it cost two old pence), some of whose early wartime advertisements make amusing reading. There was a local dairy whose proprietor was G D Stephens, but by chance it happened to be called Carpenter's Dairy. Should parishioners favour the dairy 'with a trial' they were assured that every effort would be made to give complete satisfaction. Indeed, families were 'waited upon twice daily.' And Bernard Smith, the pharmacist in Weymouth Street, announced that prescriptions were 'dispensed with the strictest accuracy.'

There was an advertisement for 'sunny holidays at Worthing' but it is doubtful whether many members of the congregation ever enjoyed a holiday anywhere. Offertories during August 1941, Edward's last year in the parish, were pitiful. Church expenses attracted three guineas;

the Woman Worker Fund, at Evensong, a mere 19s 5d, but perhaps the congregation felt they had done their bit by contributing £3 0s 1d to the Air Raid Distress Fund in the morning. One can just imagine the embarrassed fumbling for pennies to put on the plate, for many of those who worshipped at Holy Trinity were truly poverty stricken. One such family somehow accommodated in a two-room basement at 138 Great Titchfield Street, rented for 8s 4d a week, consisted of Albert and Alice Wright and their six children.

Alice Wright lost one baby, and those who survived, two boys and four girls, were born at three yearly intervals, the second girl and third child, Lilian Betsy, born in 1917, recalling in later life how she was sent out to buy stale bread and cracked eggs. If it is true, as Lilian claims, that her earliest recollection is of her father shaking in terror when a German zeppelin flew overhead, it may well account for her amazingly retentive memory and her ability to recall the past in vivid detail. She remembers how her father would play all the popular tunes of the day on a mouth organ, but how he only brought it out when he had had a few drinks. Although her father would kiss all the children each day when he left for work, Lilian says she cannot ever remember being kissed by her mother. 'My home was only secure when sister Alice [the eldest of the family] came in.' There was no running water and the family shared a lavatory in the back yard with tenants on the ground floor, one of whom was a prostitute. Lilian's pocket money was ½d a week, with which she tried to buy sweets 'that lasted a long time.'

Lilian's mother had been born in Neal Street, Covent Garden, her own mother having been in domestic service. She says: 'The family cut my mother off because she had let herself go.' Of Irish extraction, Alice Wright 'found it quite impossible to manage,' and the emotional scars of a maternally deprived childhood never really healed; in old age Lilian will catch herself describing her mother as 'a bit of a slut, no doubt about it', only to repent when her natural reserves of charity enable her to adjust the critical balance. She says she can only once recall her mother crying, on the occasion of her own brother's death, but Lilian herself was so prone to crying that the family called her water melon. Compared to the Carpenters, into whose family Lilian would one day marry, life for the Wrights in Great Titchfield Street must at times have been a nightmare. All the children were delivered in the basement, by a lady called Mrs Church, who claimed to be a midwife. Lilian remembers, 'All she asked for was newspaper and hot water, and she charged half a crown. Sometimes I was sent to her to borrow a shilling.'

Lilian's grandfather Albert originally worked in Covent Garden as a porter. During the Great War her father was employed at the Woolwich

Arsenal, and after the war he set up in business as a shoe repairer, but how he acquired the skill no one knows. Lilian's elder brother Ted picked up the trade from watching his father at work and was obviously a boy with keen perceptions, for it seems he learnt the classical music repertoire listening to a crystal set. Lilian says she was always hungry as a child, and she must have been sorely tempted to eat some of her father's lunch, which she delivered to him still, amazingly enough, piping hot, although his shop was quite a walk away. It was a wonder too that the stew her mother had prepared was still on the plate, for Lilian would always run anywhere rather than walk. Her father would sometimes have a boiled egg for breakfast, into which the children were allowed to have a dip, but their staple diet was bread and dripping. 'There was never anything in the kitchen cupboard,' Lilian recalls. 'We simply lived from hand to mouth.'

There were times when the rent was in arrears, for at either end of the street was a pub, to one of which Lilian's mother would now and again repair with a jug to collect some ale, dipping a red hot poker into the beer on her return home. But she doesn't sound a bad sort in many ways; somehow she managed to provide a cooked meal every day, and in the winter there was always a fire. 'She didn't keep us very clean,' says Lilian (there was no bath), 'but she took in washing. She was very good when we were ill but she wasn't a bit interested in what we did at school.' Her parents, she says, 'rubbed along together.' They never had a holiday or closed the shop, and their Sunday recreation was a visit to the West End to gaze in the glittering shop windows.

Lilian loved going to school, where what she most enjoyed was poetry, much of it engraved on her memory for life. At the age of 10 she was quite seriously ill, only weighed four stone, and was sent to Broadstairs to recuperate. On her return home she found her Brownie uniform had been pawned. Some of her happiest childhood memories are of visits to nearby Regent's Park, fortified by jam sandwiches wrapped in newspaper. When she was 14 she was sent out to work, for the Wrights were more concerned to increase their precarious income than to produce well-educated children. Her first job was with a firm of dyers and cleaners; her salary was a useful 10 shillings a week. At 17 she was employed as a match girl by a firm of milliners in Margaret Street called 'Vogue's Veils'. Until this time the four girls had shared a bed in the front room while the two boys shared a bed in the kitchen, where their parents also slept. The lack of privacy, for the parents and for the children when they were adolescent, must have been reminiscent of life in the London tenements of Dickens's day, and the facts of life came as no surprise to the Wright children. In this respect, Lilian may have been more precocious than Edward, whose school days were spent as a day boy. Lilian and her brothers and sisters only returned home to eat and sleep, Lilian's preferred environment being the street, where she joined in the boys' games whenever she could and 'skipped by the hour'. Only too conscious of the class and financial divide between her rundown eighteenth century street and houses of a similar vintage around the corner belonging to affluent middle class families, Lilian developed a compensatory fantasy world in which her neighbours became her loyal subjects. It is hardly surprising that when, as the wife of a canon, and eventually dean, of Westminster, she met royalty she tended to treat them as absolute equals, as did Edward.

In order to get some peace and quiet at the weekend, many parents sent their children to Sunday School; Lilian was one such, and the parish church, Holy Trinity, became in many ways the centre of her life. It provided a foundation stone, and because of her links with a busy Christian community, and despite her family's poverty, she remembers only 'the richest childhood', the streets still ringing with vendors' cries and the parish providing a communal life and a sense of worth. Lilian's horizons were further expanded when she was 17, for the family moved to rented accommodation in Camden, with rooms looking out on a garden with a tree, a luxury the memory of which she savours to this day. One year later - in 1935 – she heard that a new curate had arrived, and she and her friends made a beeline for Holy Trinity to investigate. Lilian, for one, was not particularly impressed. Edward Carpenter would never have pretended to cut a romantic figure – he was far too studious looking for that – and he was wearing a rather shapeless yellow cardigan which became ever more shapeless the more he tugged at it. When Lilian heard him preach things were no better; intellectually he stood head and shoulders above the congregation, and he had not yet learned to modify his imagery, although the Rector did his best to rein him in.

Edward was living on the first floor of the clergy house at 74 Bolsover Street. His fellow occupants, not themselves clergy but whose rents were a welcome addition to the church's income, included a journalist, a medical student, a musician much fawned over by the ladies, and at weekends an organist, William Tubbs, who otherwise lived at Haywards Heath. Many of these men remained friends throughout Edward's life. There was a communal dining room, and tenants were charged for meals according to the number of courses they ate. Those feeling particularly impecunious would surfeit themselves on soup and bread. Memorable children's parties were held at the clergy house, which served also as a meeting place for many of Edward's academic and literary contemporaries.

Wearing a homberg, Edward began to meet Lilian for lunch, a shared devotion to poetry being the catalyst that brought them together. Having drifted away from her own family, Lilian began to satisfy her maternal instincts by training in a children's hospital, St Mary's, Carshalton Beeches, and to this day she mourns the death of a boy of eleven on her ward. Having failed her written exam, Lilian switched her attention to the Guildhall School of Music and Drama, Edward somehow managing to pay her fees. In 1938, when Lilian was 21 and Edward 27, they became engaged. He bought her an amethyst ring, which later she lost; she seems to have had a penchant for mislaying valuable items, and gives the impression of not really being attached to objects any more than Edward was. One also gets the strong impression that Edward did not find the ritual of wooing very congenial; the engagement was to last three years. Lilian recalled that the first she learnt of Edward's serious intentions towards her was when an elderly female parishioner interrupted them reading poetry alone together in Edward's rooms in the Clergy House. She commented on the impropriety of such an arrangement, to which Edward responded by saying, 'Do you think I would have invited Miss Wright to read poetry in my room if I did not intend to marry her?' Edward tended to express his emotional feelings in poetry rather than by verbal communication, his love poems being heavily influenced by the Romantic movement, to which he felt so closely drawn.

8 June 1937 found Edward setting to verse a wistful longing for Devon, its rivers, lanes, fields and churches, but the last stanza recalls:

> My Devonshire girl is London born
> Where life is dirty, and life forlorn
> But a country girl she is to me
> Child of the fields, the wind, the sea.

The year of their engagement saw quite a spate of love lyrics dedicated to Lilian or inspired by her. He also wrote at this time a rather charming series of poems about children, inspired by his knowledge of two little boys Lilian was looking after, called David and Michael. One surely need look no further for an explanation of his choice of names for his own first two boys. The surrogate David was honoured with a two verse effort:

> Mummy shall I one day be a star
> And twinkle in the night
> And will you see me from afar
> And say, 'That's David's light.'
>
> I'd love to - oh, but mummy dear
> If I should go so far
> I couldn't leave you lonely here
> So you must be a star.

It would seem that by the autumn of 1939 Edward's thoughts were seriously turning in the direction of a teaching appointment, perhaps one that combined a chaplaincy, for on 18 September that year George Saywell furnished him with a reference for use as and when required. 'The Rev E F Carpenter has worked with me as assistant Curate for the last four years. This parish is an evacuated area, which means that much of Mr Carpenter's work has ceased. He is a man of wide learning and of brilliant intellectual gifts, and is supremely a teacher. He has always taken an interest in the young people of this parish and has proved himself to be a real leader of the young. He has an attractive personality and makes easy contacts with people of all types and all ages.

'I am sure that his exceptional gifts would be an asset to any school, and I most warmly and sincerely recommend him for such a post.'

With the outbreak of war the parish magazine began to run a feature called The Sentinel Circle, a 'Readers' Forum for Exchanging Useful Personal Experience in Home Affairs.' It may be doubted whether the future Mrs Edward Carpenter needed tips on 'a good cake to make without eggs,' nor advice on how to 'repair a slit in an oilskin umbrella' - by saving 'all adhesive tape when opening tins.' Young wives were also advised never to throw away the husks of green peas; they were to turn them into green pea soup. Disaster struck in May 1941 when the clergy house was bombed, and Edward lost all his possessions save the thesis he was writing for his doctorate of philosophy, which he had the savvy to keep always with him. When Edward did not turn up to take a service the next morning, the assumption was that he was dead or injured – but he had been sleeping elsewhere. Lilian also described arriving at Bolsover Street to meet Edward the morning after the bomb and fearing the worst when she saw the destroyed clergy house.

The outbreak of war in 1939 had coincided with the aged Winnington-Ingram finally being persuaded to retire. His place as bishop of London was taken by the Bishop of Chester, a former headmaster of Repton. Schoolmasterly and dictatorial, he was to play a major if posthumous role in Edward's career, for one of the gigantic tasks taken on by Edward when he was archdeacon of Westminster was the authorship of Geoffrey Fisher's second, and by far most comprehensive, biography. Their paths first crossed when in 1941 Edward felt it was time (the time was overdue, in fact) for him to experience a second assistant curacy, and it cannot have been entirely by chance that he gravitated towards St Mary's, Harrow-on-the-Hill; Byron had been a boy at the school and spent many dreamy hours in the churchyard surveying the Middlesex plain 400 feet below, the churchyard in which one day his daughter Allegra would be buried. Even the Harrow telephone exchange was Byron.

Although still only engaged, Edward and Lilian were inspected by the churchwardens, who very grandly entertained them to dinner at Le Coq d'Or, one of Piccadilly's most expensive and fashionable restaurants, the meal beginning, however, at the distinctly unfashionable hour of 6.30pm and going on until midnight. (Le Coq d'Or continued to flourish after the war but has long since been closed down.) Edward's first meeting with the vicar, an old Harrovian by the name of Edgar Stogden, was even more incongruous. It appears they discussed nothing but cricket, Stogden advising against any mention from the pulpit of politics or religion on the grounds that such subjects were too controversial. In the event, one of the parishioners, Millicent Harris, who kept in touch with Edward until very near the end of his life, has recalled that he was 'a very clear preacher and did not display any noticeable eccentricities.'[2] Edgar Stogden, on the other hand, most certainly did. He lived alone in a large vicarage and rode round the parish on horseback throwing a fistful of pebbles at the front door if he wanted to speak to a parishioner; he seldom entered a house if he could help it as he was terrified of illness and therefore never visited the sick. Fisher was anxious for Edward to try and help him ease Stogden out of the living, a desire Fisher must have shared with the churchwardens, which would explain the most unusual occurrence of them meeting up with someone ostensibly applying to become only a curate.

Stogden was eventually succeeded as vicar of St Mary's by a holder of the Victoria Cross, the Reverend G H Woolley, and during the interregnum before Woolley arrived Edward officially held the fort; but he found himself more or less running the parish from the start, for most of the first year without a wife by his side.[3] Stogden wrote to Edward from the vicarage in Harrow on 22 August 1941 to say he hoped he could join the parish in October. Six days later he was writing: 'I very much hope you will be able to come, for I feel I should be very happy with you. What I particularly want is a good preacher, and a nice man - and I know you are both.

'My churchmanship is "central", with a leaning to "high" - and I am presuming that would fit in with yours.' (Edward had no 'leanings' towards high churchmanship; his churchmanship was strictly what was then known as Central Church.) Stodgen added a postscript: 'I can't quite read the name of your house!' and he would not have been the first, or the last, person to find Edward's handwriting a trial. On 17 November, by which time Edward was installed as assistant curate, Stogden was writing, 'Dear Carpenter (If I may leave out the Mr - which will I hope be "Dr" soon), I should be grateful if you would give a miss to any idea of Choral Celebration. We had been through it all some time ago. And had made some experiments, and I don't at all want the subject brought up again now. The High Church element were quite nice about it all … but it is a most tiring disagreement to have to settle. The main point in church life is to work harmoniously together, and I feel there has always been friendly agreement here in the parish, which is largely central without much inclination to High Church. I don't want all the arguments brought up again now - my hat, there are plenty of difficulties without that! I feel you will be a very soothing influence in certain quarters. Nearly all our people are extremely nice.'

The idea that a choral celebration of the Eucharist was in any true sense 'high church' was a curious notion; incense and vestments would have been required for that to be the case. At all events, Stogden went on to thank Edward for the sermon he had preached the day before - his first at Harrow, presumably. It had been 'a very good subject' with 'perfect phrasing, and just the right length.' He added, 'I hear the children very much enjoyed your pastoral address.' It was not unusual for clergy in the same parish to communicate by letter; when Mervyn Stockwood, later bishop of Southwark, became vicar of Great St Mary's, Cambridge in 1955 he would cajole, admonish and encourage his curates by stuffing lengthy letters in their cubbyholes in the vestry rather than confront them with criticisms and instructions face to face. Evidently at this time Edward was also helping George Saywell, taking matins and evensong on 28 December. 'Tell him you are worth your weight in gold to me,' Stogden instructed Edward, adding '(What you get comes out of my pocket!)' Early in January 1942, however, links with Marylebone were finally severed, Saywell sending Edward - as he now addressed him - a leaving present of £32 15s 6d from the parish.[4] (In the same year, 1942, George Saywell was appointed an honorary prebendary of St Paul's and in 1944 he became rector of St Michael's, Cornhill. Four years later he was appointed a chaplain to the king. He died in 1956 at the age of 74.)

Lilian Carpenter has described 1941 as 'a very difficult year.' Following the destruction of the Marylebone clergy house, and before moving to Harrow, Edward was living rough in the church while trying to complete his thesis; Lilian had a job running a Play Centre in Ladbroke Grove and was beginning to wonder if she would spend the rest of her life looking after other people's children, for Edward seemed in no hurry to get married. He was, says Lilian, 'psychologically in a very low state,' and by now she was having to fend off other suitors. But she felt, she says, that God wanted her to take on Edward.

Lilian reported having finally to give Edward an ultimatum. Either they were to marry soon, or she would take a job in Scotland. In the end the marriage could not have got off to a more surreal start. On 10 December 1941 Edward doubled back to Holy Trinity where he and Lilian were married, at 11.30am, virtually in secret, with only two witnesses present. On his wedding day Edward went out and bought a whistle, to referee a football match, and by 3pm that afternoon he was conducting a study circle in Harrow, the subject of their deliberations being 'Whether an eternity of pain or punishment is compatible with a wholly beneficent creator.' Lilian was left to make her own way to the house in Harrow where Edward was living. As he had not thought to warn his housekeeper of her pending arrival Lilian was somewhat disconcerted when the housekeeper asked who she was. 'I'm Mrs Carpenter,' she explained. 'But he's not married' was the welcome she received.

Three

STANMORE

A Norman door on the west side of St Mary's, Harrow-on-the-Hill remains the only external clue to its ancient origins; in 1094 the church was consecrated by St Anselm just a year after he had become the thirty-sixth archbishop of Canterbury. Most of the chancel was rebuilt in the nineteenth century by George Gilbert Scott, not entirely to the satisfaction of that connoisseur of ecclesiastical architecture, John Betjeman, who thought Scott's restoration too fierce and the general appearance of the church hard within and flinty without. But on his appointment as assistant curate at the end of 1941 Edward Carpenter would have found much to please the eye from previous periods; a fifteenth century roof in the nave, for instance, and a richly carved seventeenth century pulpit. Placed on such an elevated promontory as it is, soaring over the sixteenth century school, Harrow itself and the surrounding countryside, the church's tall octagonal spire has served as a signpost. In 1999 St Mary's found its way into Simon Jenkins's masterly England's Thousand Best Churches.[1]

It is by no means uncommon for a clergyman to find himself the unwitting recipient of besotted devotion on the part of a female member of his congregation. It at first appeared that such a fate had befallen Edward at Harrow, when a middle aged spinster, Winifred Hornby, purchased a house at Kenton as a home for herself and her widowed father. It was not long before Winifred, a rather sad and lonely person, had attached herself to St Mary's, and in particular to the assistant curate, who kindly invited her home to tea. From an account of this relationship sent to the author by a former work colleague of Winifred's it would seem that Edward became nervous about the degree of devotion he had engendered in Winifred, who noticed a certain cooling off in his friendship. 'He told her that once there was a girl who had a crush on him, and when she realised he was offering a strictly platonic association she had committed suicide. So now he was always very careful if he became friendly with a lady.'[2]

As far as Winifred Hornby was concerned, however, Edward had got completely the wrong end of the stick. 'Sharply, W H responded, "It is not men who attract me but women!" and immediately Dr C reverted to his former warmth towards her.'

Lilian Carpenter recalls how Winifred followed Edward to his next parish, Stanmore, where she was firmly told he could only see her once a month, and eventually to Westminster Abbey, where she became in fact a regular guest on Sundays. After Sunday lunch, she did secretarial work for Edward and would type letters for him. Her talents were small; she sang in a couple of amateur choirs and entertained vague ambitions to become a writer, and in so far as he was able, Edward tried to encourage her. She was typically a disturbed person in need of relationships to compensate for an unhappy childhood and an unfulfilled adult existence whom many people would have shaken off, but when Edward died Winifred's former friend wrote to Lilian to say, 'As far as I know, you and your family (she often mentioned your children) constituted the only permanent, loving relationship in a long, sad and painful life. The rest of the people she knew, myself included, failed her, but the Carpenter family were the only people who treated her with kindness and friendliness.'

'I hear a rumour that you are going to Stanmore,' Edward's former vicar, Edgar Stogden, wrote to him on 10 October 1944 from his new home at Northwood, a few miles north-west of Harrow. 'Best congratulations, though I am jolly sorry you are leaving Harrow. It had to come soon on your journey upwards, which won't stop till you get near the top..! I was always very grateful for the good work you did for me, and for your loyalty. There is big work to be done at Stanmore; you will find very nice people there, and Bernays knew how to bind them to himself in a wonderful way. Your lady will like it there – and please give her my best wishes, and many thanks for the work she did at the clubs when she had so much to do elsewhere.'

Prebendary Stewart Bernays had been appointed Rector of St John the Evangelist, Great Stanmore in 1898, and he and his wife were responsible for the church's First World War memorial. Now their son Robert Bernays, member of parliament for Bristol North since 1931 (he had been elected at the age of 29 and had already held several junior posts), was patron of the living. On 1 August 1944 he had written to Edward to say that when he preached at Stanmore he had made a great impression and there was a strong body on the Parochial Church Council 'who I know would very much like to have you.' The living, he told Edward, was worth 'about £800 a year'. There was 'a delightful old Rectory,' and the finances of the church were 'in first class order.' Captain Bernays believed that Stanmore was likely to expand greatly after the war, and he was sure there was 'a great field of service there.' Would Edward like him to consider his name for the benefice?

Three days later, writing from Horfield Barracks in Bristol (he had enlisted in 1943 and was now commissioned in the Royal Engineers)

Bernays told Edward he was very glad to hear that he was willing to discuss 'the possibilities of Stanmore.' He suggested a meeting in London, not at his club, which was closed, but at the Carlton Grill. 'Would Mrs Carpenter care to join us?' he enquired. 'Please tell her that I would be delighted if she would do so.' Lilian recalled that Bernays spent the entire meal talking to her, and at the end turned to Edward and offered him the living of Great Stanmore. As they left the Carlton Grill, Lilian turned to Edward and said, 'I got you that job!' Bernays warned the Carpenters that Stanmore Rectory, 'is a bit of an undertaking,' and admitted that there were 'household problems that would be involved in taking over!' Problems was putting it mildly. When eventually the Carpenters did move into the Rectory Edward's father had to be roped in to help with repairs and decorating. In 1949 Edward and Lilian had to endure the disruption of the Rectory being divided into two houses, as a result of which the interior was very much spoilt. A year after they left deathwatch beetles were found to be devouring the eighteenth century timbers, and a new Rectory was eventually built in 1960.

By 21 August Robert Bernays was writing to Edward to make a formal offer of the living. 'I have consulted with the Bishop of London who approves of my decision to make you this offer,' he reassured Edward, although there were stories that Fisher was furious, preferring that Edward should serve in the East End. And by the beginning of September, having also been assured by Bernays he had reason to believe his appointment would commend itself to the PCC, Edward, serving as priest-in-charge at St Mary's, had accepted. 'I know that you will find a very warm welcome,' Bernays wrote on 2 September. 'I cannot wish you more than that you and your wife should find the same happiness at the Rectory as did my Father and Mother a quarter of a century ago.' It may safely be assumed that the Carpenters' time spent at Stanmore was indeed a happy one; it witnessed the birth of their first two children, David on Christmas Eve 1946 and Michael on 11 April 1949.

Parishioners were informed in their Stanmore Church and Village Magazine, in an article signed HSG (he was the lay Reader, Harold Goodwin, who had alerted the patron of the living to Edward's abilities in the pulpit), that it had not at first been Edward's intention to take Holy Orders; that at the age of 14 he had thought of going to Wye Agricultural College 'to learn to be a farmer.' Presumably Edward had sanctioned this information, although the date of his first curacy was wrong by a year. In case Mr Goodwin's readers feared that Edward's intellectual attainments might frighten them off they were informed that he played tennis and delighted in cycling, hiking, camps, plays and debates. With his myopic eyesight, Edward was to become an alarmingly familiar figure weaving his charmed course through the London traffic on a bicycle.

Edward was to be instituted and inducted by the suffragan bishop of Willesden and the archdeacon of Hampstead on 3 February 1945 as the 38th Rector of St John the Evangelist, where the liturgical worship would have suited him perfectly; there was an 8am celebration of Holy Communion on Sunday with a Choral Eucharist at 9am twice a month, Morning Prayer at 11am and Evensong at six. There was one weekly celebration of Holy Communion, at 10.30am on Tuesday, and Evensong was said daily at 5.30pm. With a Children's Service every Sunday afternoon and a Sunday School run by Lilian he was expected to manage on his own, initially at any rate. Captain Bernays had told Edward he hoped to be present at his induction, but since taking off from Rome on 23 January the plane in which he and another MP were making for Brindisi had gone missing. Bernays' death was eventually confirmed, and listed as 'June 1945'.

The church entrusted to Edward had been consecrated in 1850 by the bishop of Salisbury, Edward Denison (consecrated at the astonishingly early age of 36), in whose diocese it most certainly did not stand. Considerable alterations to the Victorian building Edward knew were made a decade after he left.

Edward's arrival at Stanmore coincided with a tragedy almost certainly responsible for a very different Church of England to the one in which he might have expected to serve his first - and only, as it transpired - spell as a parish priest. On 26 October 1944, just as Edward was in the process of moving from Harrow to Stanmore, and only two and a half years after leaving York for Canterbury, one of the great charismatic figures of the twentieth century, William Temple, suddenly died. With a touch of hyperbole, perhaps, a young radical priest, later to become famous as Rector of St Mary-le-Bow in Cheapside, Joseph McCulloch, declared at Temple's funeral, 'We are burying the hopes of the Church of England.'[3] The Provost of Queen's College, Oxford, R H Hodgkin, thought that Temple's death 'seemed to shake the Western world as if one of its pillars had been removed.'[4] Temple, the son of another archbishop of Canterbury, Frederick Temple, had been appointed headmaster of Repton at the age of 29. He was a socialist and a philosophical theologian, so he would have been very much a man after Edward's own heart. As bishop of Manchester and then archbishop of York he had become a legend in his lifetime. 'Prodigal in his gifts, lavish in his generosity, wide in his interests, abundant in his energy, holy in his dedication' is how Edward himself was to describe William Temple when in 1971 he published one of his most important books, Cantuar: The Archbishops in their Office. Renowned for his leadership of the Life and Liberty Movement, and remembered for calling, as early as 1917, for freedom for the Church from the 'intolerable hindrance' of parliamentary control, it was widely anticipated that Temple would guide the Church of England with a sure and prophetic touch through the difficult years of post-war reconstruction.

There were two leading contenders to take Temple's place at Canterbury, Geoffrey Fisher, bishop of London since 1939, and George Bell, bishop of Chichester since 1929. As Bell had courageously spoken out against the indiscriminate bombing of essentially civilian targets like Dresden he never entertained any serious chance of preferment, not even to London, so long as Churchill remained prime minister. Churchill had no serious interest in Church appointments or knowledge of the people involved - except, of course, when they brought themselves to his attention by annoying him; he was content to receive advice from people like Brendon Bracken, who would only put forward names they knew to be innocuous. During his time as bishop of London, Fisher had relished his gifts for administration, and he was invited to 10 Downing Street for a lunch that clinched the matter. He would spend much of his considerable energy and ability (he was a Triple First) on administration while at Canterbury, in particular revising canon law. There had been grave concern during the war about recruitment of ordinands, and the dean of St Paul's, W R Matthews, came to believe after the war that the bishops and clergy 'worked hard on canon law when the future of the Church became day by day more precarious.' He went so far as to compare the bishops' time-consuming engagement in the revision of canon law to 'a man who occupied himself in rearranging the furniture when the house was on fire.'

Quite by chance, it was not long before Edward had neighbouring clergy destined to become distinguished bishops, and in the case of one of them a colleague also at Westminster Abbey. In 1947 George Appleton, in 1963 appointed archbishop of Perth and six years later archbishop in Jerusalem, became vicar of Headstone, near Harrow. And the following year a wealthy and flamboyant Anglo-Catholic, Joost de Blank, archbishop of Cape Town from 1957 to 1963 and a canon of Westminster from 1964 to 1968, took up residence as vicar of St John the Baptist, Greenhill. Four years later he was consecrated suffragan bishop of Stepney. Joost and his mother, who lived with him, gave welcome parties for the rural deanery.

One of Edward's most famous parishioners was the wartime deputy prime minister, Clement Attlee. Within months of Edward's arrival the country had dismissed Winston Churchill from office, Labour enjoyed a landslide victory, and their leader, Attlee, and his family moved into 10 Downing Street. Attlee's daughter, Lady Felicity Harwood, recalls Edward's arrival at Stanmore 'as a young man with auburn curls.' They were all so delighted to have him as their rector she reminded Lilian when

writing on 1 September 1998 to commiserate on Edward's death. Lady
Felicity married a divorcee and was obliged to undergo a register office
ceremony, but Edward held a service of blessing for the couple. Attlee,
one of whose duties as prime minister was to recommend ecclesiastical
crown appointments to the King, never attended church, but Lady Felicity
says that Edward was 'a wonderful change after his predecessor, Hewett,
who was rather a ponderous man.'[5] William Hewett had been at Stanmore
21 years and was now 75, which did not prevent him moving on to
Greensted, near Ongar, where he remained incumbent until the age of 85.
Edward married Attlee's younger daughter as well as other members of
the family, and by 1949 he was in receipt of the official Attlee Christmas
card, complete with photograph. The start of his career at Westminster
Abbey was to be a direct result of his Stanmore friendship with the
Labour prime minister.

Bishop Say believes that Edward 'was at his best in terms of family
crisis, as my wife and I experienced when our first son died within a week
of his birth and was buried by Edward in the churchyard at Stanmore.'[6] In
the pulpit, the new Rector's sermons - 'very scholarly, spiced liberally not
only with Biblical quotations (especially from the Gospels and St Paul's
letters) but also with quotations from philosophers such as Plato' - made
an indelible impression on the head choirboy, 13-year-old Robert Lee.
He was not alone in his appreciation of Edward's preaching. Apparently
Merlyn Rees, in later life a cabinet minister, used to walk every Sunday
evening from Hatch End, which actually is not very far, to listen to the
sermon. Young Robert was one of the first Stanmore parishioners Edward
prepared for Confirmation, and he has particular cause to remember
the new Rector with affection, for shortly after his arrival he engaged
a professional organist and choirmaster, and took the boys on camping
expeditions; he also raised the choirboys' pay from 6s 6d a quarter to
10s 6d. Robert Lee was also a good example of a young churchgoer so
influenced by his parish priest that he remained not only a friend but was
drawn to seek ordination. In 1953 he became a 21-year-old godfather to
the Carpenters' third son, Paul.

Lilian also threw herself into the activities of the parish. Most notably,
following her drama studies at the Guildhall she began to direct and
produce a series of plays with the children of the parish – to much acclaim.
The last of these, an open-air production of A Midsummer Night's Dream,
was performed just after she and Edward had left for the Abbey, but she
returned for the performances and David remembers watching from the
round window of the Stanmore Rectory as the torches of the fairies lit up
the darkness.

Midway through Edward's time at Stanmore, in 1948, SPCK published (again for the Church Historical Society) the thesis that had earned him his PhD; *Thomas Tenison; His Life and Times*. Tenison was born in 1636, and survived into the first year of the Hanovarian succession. Weighed down with learned, prodigious research, like *Thomas Sherlock* this was scarcely a biography for the general reader, quite apart from Edward's consistent academic tendency, for example, to write 'Charles had been now some nineteen years returned from his travels.' As a political, never mind ecclesiastical, account of the seventeenth century, however, the book has to remain a cornerstone of gathered knowledge. It was dedicated to the Regius Professor of Ecclesiastical History at Oxford, and to Dr Norman Sykes, Dixie Professor of Ecclesiastical History at Cambridge, Professor Sykes having supervised Edward's studies. It may well have been in the wake of publication of this impressive tome that Edward was invited to preach at St Paul's Cathedral.

As a parish priest, Edward believed he should spend his mornings in his study and his afternoons visiting - which he did at Stanmore on a motor scooter. And throughout his long ministry at Westminster Abbey he struck many people as essentially a parish priest at heart, believing there was no clerical position that involved greater responsibility. No matter what pressure he was under, a plea for help from an equally hard-pressed parish priest would find Edward speeding on his way to lend a hand. When eventually he became dean of Westminster he would remark that the parish clergy had a challenge to get people to come to church whereas the challenge he faced was knowing what to do with the people who flocked to the Abbey in such numbers.

And parish visiting was never short of surprises. In a nursing home Edward discovered an aged nanny employed in the past by Marina, Duchess of Kent, whom Edward persuaded to suppress her memoirs. At 10 Elm Park in Stanmore Edward unearthed a great-niece of the poet Wordsworth, who gave him a cheque for three guineas with which to buy a hat when he went to Westminster. The historian in him was naturally excited to discover that not only had her father been bishop of St Andrew's but in 1828 had rowed in the first University Boat Race, and had been Gladstone's private tutor at Oxford. She told Edward she had dined with a dean of Salisbury who, as a boy in Scotland, had met an old man who had held the Stuart Pretender's horse at Culloden. She was still writing chatty letters to Edward nine years after he had left the parish, one of them having been horribly stained on receipt with tea or coffee. Edward was to bury Mary Wordsworth one month short of her 100th birthday, and in her will she left Lilian a diamond brooch, which she swapped for the old lady's childhood Bible, bequeathed to someone else. For some reason perhaps best left unexplained, Lilian still possesses Mary Wordsworth's tea cosy. On the subject of links with the past, one of Edward's great-grandmothers died at the age of 101, having been born before the French Revolution, and Edward's father could remember her saying, when in a fit of temper he threw a knife at his brother Ted, 'If you go on like that you'll end up on the gallows!'

In the summer of 1950 celebrations for the centenary of the Victorian church building were held, and Edward invited the Attlees to a service to be held on 17 July, but he was told by Violet Attlee, who addressed him as 'Dear Rector', she would be glad to attend but that it was quite impossible for her husband to do so. 'Nowadays,' she wrote from 10 Downing Street, 'he cannot take any engagements during the week.' And already the Carpenters' stay in Stanmore was drawing to a close. In 1941 one of the canons at Westminster Abbey, Russell Barry, had been consecrated bishop of Southwell, and the canonry had remained unfilled. On 8 April 1949 Sir Anthony Bevir, the prime minister's appointments secretary, had written to Edward to say, 'Your name has been brought to the notice of the Prime Minister in connection with patronage in his gift,' and enclosed was a form Edward was asked to fill in. There was at this stage no clue about the possible patronage that might be forthcoming, other than the obvious fact that his name was being docketed for future consideration for a crown appointment. At 40 Edward would have been young to have been considered for a diocesan bishopric, and the prime minister had nothing to do with choosing suffragans. Certainly no deanery would have been offered to someone of Edward's age. A stall in a cathedral, however, remained a distinct possibility. Edward later recalled that Attlee had asked him, 'would you prefer Westminster or St Paul's?'

Edward was now certainly under surveillance. On 2 August 1950 Charles Smyth, a residentiary canon at Westminster and since 1946 Rector of St Margaret's, wrote to Edward to say, 'I have long been an admirer of your studies in ecclesiastical biography, & should be very pleased if you would care to preach in the Abbey on Sunday *Oct 29th* at *3.0 Evensong*. I hope that you can manage this. I should perhaps add that the Abbey congregation is not particularly "highbrow" or scholarly, though they can appreciate scholarship if presented in popular language & in a fairly simple form. This I know to be within your compass.' Canon Smyth was wise to underline the date and time; Edward's diary could sometimes contain only the very vaguest hints about appointments.

And now, marking his letter Confidential, as is customary, on 10 November Clement Attlee was writing to the Rector of Stanmore to say:

My dear Carpenter, The King has given approval for the revival of the Fifth Canonry at Westminster Abbey, which was suspended during the war, and it is my duty to make a recommendation of a name to His Majesty to fill this appointment.

I should explain that, though in the past the parish of St John, Smith Square, was attached to this Canonry, a Scheme for disannexation is now in its final stages.

Until His Majesty's approval has been obtained, I trust that you will treat this proposal as confidential.

Edward Carpenter was that rare combination, a pastor and a scholar. He had gained 15 years experience of parish work, meeting what we are pleased to call ordinary people, and displaying an enviable ability to love and understand pretty well everyone he met. But the offer of a residentiary canonry carried the promise of time away from routine parish duties in which to study and write. Two weeks after writing to offer Edward a stall at Westminster Attlee was again in communication, a letter having gone from Edward to Attlee on 20 November accepting the offer. On 27 November (Edward's birthday) Attlee wrote to say:

My dear Carpenter, I write to inform you that the King has been graciously pleased to approve your appointment to the Fifth Canonry at Westminster Abbey.

I am confident that you will justify the choice that His Majesty has made.

It was all a wonderful fiction. It is most unlikely that George VI had ever heard of Edward Carpenter, let alone made a personal choice. Although Westminster Abbey is a Royal Peculiar, and the Sovereign is the Abbey's Visitor, when it comes to appointments to the Chapter the monarch acts on the advice of the prime minister. It was a bit of luck that at any rate Attlee knew Edward, for there is no guarantee that had he taken soundings from his appointments secretary some other name might not have been put forward. When a long view is taken of Edward's 34 years spent at the Abbey, the Church has much for which to thank an astute if non-churchgoing prime minister.

At least by this time the dean, Alan Don, had been consulted by Downing Street - but only in relation to the timing of the announcement. It is one of the crazy anomalies of Anglican Church life - or it certainly was until very recently - that the Dean and Chapter, while possibly asked for their opinion of the sort of person required to fill a vacancy, have no say in who is actually foisted on them, such a ludicrous state of affairs so often leading to incompatible teams being assembled. As it transpired that Alan Don, appointed to the deanery in 1946, considered 'it desirable that the announcement should be made with as little delay as possible,' Edward would have needed to alert his bishop and parishioners of his pending departure without any delay at all.

Edward had in fact written to the dean on 20 November, the day he wrote to the prime minister, to tell him he had accepted the canonry. Three days later the dean explained to Edward: 'I would have written before now had it not been that a debate in the House of Commons on Friday morning made reference to the vacant Canonry, with the result that I have been in communication with the Prime Minister about it and have urged him to proceed with the appointment...' He wrote again on 1 December, having been 'laid up for a day or two with an abscess in the jaw,' to say he had written to the Bishop of London (since Fisher's translation to Canterbury, William Wand) 'thanking him for what he had done to accelerate the promotion of the scheme whereby the canonry was disannexed from St John's, Smith Square, and commiserating with him on the loss of one of his clergy.' The dean added, 'He seems gratified that the appointment should have gone to one of his parish priests, while at the same time deploring your departure from the diocese.' As a Royal Peculiar, the Abbey was of course outside any episcopal jurisdiction.

It now only necessitated a farewell party, at which Edward was presented with a cheque for £187. He and Lilian also both received a gold watch (which Lilian lost and Edward kept), the Young People's Fellowship came up with a table lamp, there were book tokens and even a teapot, and finally Lilian was presented with a cameo brooch by her pupils in the Sunday School. Such largesse was a far cry from her impoverished days as a humble parishioner in Marylebone.

Four

CANONS ANCIENT AND MODERN

Edward Carpenter was 10 when he paid his first visit to Westminster Abbey, and when he came to write a popular history of the Abbey in retirement he had no difficulty recalling his childhood reaction. 'Alas! It was an impression of sepulchral and unrelieved gloom.'[1] The dust had well and truly settled both inside and out, and not a lot had changed in 30 years by the time Edward, aged 40, and Lilian moved into No 2 Little Cloister. David was four, Michael just two, and both boys, together with their brother Paul, born in 1953, and sister Louise, born in 1960, were to spend their entire childhoods in the supposedly cloistered calm of a great medieval abbey. There was, however, a perpetual bustle; Westminster schoolboys provided the boisterous atmosphere of a county rugby ground, the cloisters, from 1979 onwards, were to draw people to their knees not to pray but to rub brasses, members of the royal family and dignitaries from overseas could be counted on to arrive almost every day, seething crowds of tourists were eventually to do their best to turn a shrine into a peepshow, and as often as not the Carpenter children's increasingly distinguished and mildly eccentric father, his eyesight never his strong point (he underwent an operation for a detached retina soon after arriving at the Abbey), would pass them by without even spotting who they were.

No 2 Little Cloister had only a small garden and Lilian made no bones about disliking it. Fortunately for the Carpenters there is a tradition at the Abbey whereby the canons move into nicer houses as the houses fall vacant and the canons acquire seniority, the absurdity of the situation being that a bachelor canon may be rattling about in a commodious house while a married canon with a family may find himself housed in less than adequate accommodation. No 2, however, had five bedrooms and two bathrooms. But apart from a recently arrived minor canon from Australia with a young family, Howard Hollis, the Carpenters had entered a stagnant world of hierarchy and snobbery, and little attention was paid to Edward's publications and outstanding achievements at King's College, London.

Edward said late in life that on his arrival he had felt 'totally bemused.' The only person who spoke to him was the Precentor, Jocelyn Perkins. They met in St Faith's Chapel, at the southern end of Poet's Corner. 'Get out of my way!' Perkins snapped. It was not long before Edward was minuting in a diary he kept spasmodically the events of a Chapter meeting. He says he was disgusted at the turning down of a proposal for a midweek lunch hour communion service. 'Both Marriott and Smyth protested against such a disastrous innovation as it would mean the possibility of unconfirmed people receiving the Sacrament!!!' At no celebration of Holy Communion can a priest ever be sure that those communicating have been confirmed. 'Adam Fox and I spoke vigorously for it but the Dean (so it seemed to me) was too timid to follow his own inclination. This is the sort of stupidity which makes me wonder why I left a parish.'

The dean, Alan Don, a Scot whose relations with his wife were such that he dined at the Athenaeum while she repaired to a Lyons Corner House, had been born in 1885 and was thus, in 1951, 66 years of age. (It is quite astonishing to read in Edward's diary, 'Shan't see the Dean till next Monday as he is burying himself this week in the Athenaeum in order to draw up his Will.') Dean Don had been educated at Rugby and Magdalen College, Oxford. At the early age of 36 he had been appointed Provost of St Paul's Cathedral, Dundee, and ten years later he made the brave decision to take a step backwards by accepting Cosmo Gordon Lang's invitation to serve as his chaplain at Lambeth. Hence by the time he was appointed to Westminster as a residentiary canon in 1941 Don was well and truly versed in the ways of the Establishment. He had held Lang's unsteady hand during the Abdication crisis and had attended the coronation of George VI in 1937. On his appointment to Westminster, Edward Carpenter was by comparison a novice in affairs of Church and State. The dean of Westminster when Don arrived had been Paul de Labilliere, educated at Harrow and Merton College, Oxford, and from 1934-37 archdeacon of Leeds and suffragan bishop of Knaresborough. He was appointed dean in 1938, listed as his sole recreation silence, and no surprise was expressed by his replacement as dean in 1946 by the worldly yet religious Alan Don. So it was odd that 28 years later there were doubts as to whether a member of the Chapter would be preferred, as Edward was. There had been, in Don, a very obvious precedent.

The sub-dean since 1944, Canon Lewis Donaldson, a pacifist and Christian Socialist who in 1905, when he was vicar of St Mark's, Leicester, had led a march of the unemployed from Leicester to London and back again, quite reasonably entertained no thoughts of succeeding Bishop de Labilliere, or anyone else for that matter. Born in 1860, he had been appointed a canon in 1924, had listened to sermons preached in Oxford by Pusey, and was now a frail but determined old man, whose ascent to the High Altar to give his blessing, declining assistance as he staggered up, could be guaranteed to keep the congregation in suspense.

More nerve wracking for his fellow clergy in the sanctuary was his insistence on administering the chalice at communion, the consecrated wine in permanent peril of being spilt, either on the carpet or over the upturned face of a communicant. If invited out to tea he and his wife would scoop any cakes left over into a paper bag.

Charles Smyth (the canon who had invited Edward to preach) and the dean were sworn enemies, and Chapter meetings went on interminably because Smyth refused to agree to anything. Apparently while working in the Abbey library on Boxing Day 1966, David Carpenter (like his father, a workaholic) took the opportunity of reading the Journals Alan Don had kept for the years 1948-53, and told his father that Don had described Charles Smyth as 'without a friend in the world.' As for the dean himself, Edward commented in his own diary, 'A D was a charmer, but his besetting sin was to take the line of least resistance ... The result was that the filibustering and bad tempered tended to get their way whereas the good tempered and accommodating were all too often sent empty away.' He thought Canon Smyth had an 'all too frequent bad temper.' The situation was eased in 1956 when Smyth took up his old fellowship at Corpus Christi, Oxford, where he settled down to write a full and frank, yet sympathetic, account of the life of Archbishop Garbett, published in 1959.

Canon Adam Fox, two years older than the dean, had arrived at the Abbey in 1942, having previously served as Warden of Radley College. He had been appointed at the early age of 35. His own education, at Winchester and University College, Oxford, had been grander even than the dean's, and from 1938 until 1943 he had held the chair of poetry at Oxford. He was living at No 4 Little Cloister, previously home to two future bishops, Charles Gore and Herbert Hensley Henson. He had a twin sister, perhaps too imaginatively named by their parents Eve, and Adam Fox told Edward that really it was he who should have been the girl for he greatly enjoyed playing with dolls and picking wild flowers. His other passion was for kippers. He remained a canon until 1963, by which time he had reached the age of 83, having celebrated his 77th birthday by riding its entire route on a No 77 London bus. He was a stickler for punctuality and disapproved of canons taking on extra-parochial work, although he had no objection to them producing works of scholarship; in 1960 he published a biography of the dean of St Paul's, W H Inge, which won the James Tait Black Memorial Prize. Fox lived on in the cloisters until he was 94, looked after initially by a housekeeper called Miss Barrs, who wore a knitted hat and suffered the appalling misfortune of having both her legs amputated. As for the old canon, he was eventually removed to a home by two well-meaning nieces, where he died. It has to be a matter of lasting regret that when his ashes were buried in Poets' Corner the Chapter funked his request for an inscription that would have read A Fox Gone to Earth.

It is incredible to think that when Edward Carpenter took up residence in 1951 there was on the staff a sub-organist, Osborne Peasgood, who had been appointed in 1924, a post he held until his death, which occurred in 1962 in the organ loft of a Welsh Presbyterian chapel in Finsbury. During the war he became acting organist and master of the choristers, but in 1946 he had to make way again for a musician of wide-ranging experience, William McKie, knighted in 1953, under whom he served loyally. Someone who arrived four years later than Peasgood (in 1928) as a minor canon, remaining in that post until 1973 (he was Sacrist from 1958 until 1973), was Christopher Hildyard. He lived discreetly for some 25 years at No 2 The Cloisters (not to be confused with the Little Cloisters) with Professor Norman Ashton, their relationship causing not so much as a raised eyebrow. Hildyard had been born at Windsor Castle, where his father was a minor canon, sang as a choirboy at the funeral of Edward VII, and had attended the coronation of George V as a page. When Edward became dean he wore a cope designed by Hildyard, who had noticed, in a shop on the Greek island of Hydra, a soldier's uniform, which he brought back to London where he had the ornamentation remounted on blue velvet. Just as Charles Smyth and Dean Don were sworn enemies, so also were Hildyard and Smyth. Hildyard in fact so despised Smyth that he found it quite impossible to include him in a painting he executed of the 1953 coronation. Such was the atmosphere in the Chapter when Edward arrived. One reason, surely, was the length of time people were permitted to serve, and then to fossilize. Jocelyn Perkins, who lived at 5 Little Cloister, had been appointed Sacrist and a minor canon two years before the death of Queen Victoria. These were the Oxbridge public school educated ecclesiastics and academics who, on their arrival, gave the Carpenters the cold shoulder. Extensive repairs and rebuilding were still going on to remedy war damage caused on the night of 10-11 May 1941 (when Alan Don took over, three of the clergy houses in Little Cloister were in ruins, the organist's house was a burnt out shell and the Deanery was also uninhabitable). The Carpenters were the first occupants of the restored No 2, and not only did Lilian consider the house 'like an institution' and 'the place full of decrepit clergy', she recalls that while Christopher Hildyard did deign to call, 'No one told us anything. Edward hadn't a clue what his duties were, what he was meant to do.'

What the Carpenters were experiencing was a last glimpse of what the Abbey must have been like 100 years before they arrived, in many ways still a place of tranquillity, where nobody bothered much about security (a situation that changed dramatically when on Christmas Eve 1950 the Stone of Scone was stolen), and where resident clergy thought of themselves as university dons, with a freehold for life. As the most junior residentiary canon, with no experience of collegiate life, Edward must have felt like the proverbial fish out of water. His one comfort, as an historian, would have been to find himself immersed in an atmosphere of almost breathtaking antiquity.

Although statutes dictate the powers and authority of the dean and canons of Westminster, as they do in any cathedral (and during the reign of Henry VIII the Abbey became the cathedral of a short-lived diocese of Westminster), at the Abbey Edward found himself for the first time since he was ordained outside any episcopal jurisdiction. Originally a Benedictine foundation, Westminster Abbey had been exempted in the Middle Ages from obedience to the bishop of London, whose diocese had been founded in the year 314, 283 years before the archbishop of Canterbury's. Instead they were to answer directly to the pope. When in 1540 the monastery was suppressed, its overlord became the king, which is why today Westminster Abbey is one of some half dozen Royal Peculiars, its most important and famous sister being St George's Chapel at Windsor. The major difference between the two is that although the sovereign remains the Abbey's Visitor, and no bishop officiates in the Abbey without the consent of the Chapter, the dean and canons are appointed by the sovereign only on the advice of the prime minister (theirs remain, in other words, crown appointments), whereas Queen Victoria made it quite clear to Gladstone in 1882 that she intended to appoint her own dean of Windsor, as indeed the Queen still does, seeking nobody's advice save that of her immediate family.

Edward's preferred historical period may have been the eighteenth century, but he was not unmoved to find himself at work in an Abbey rebuilt in the thirteenth century by Henry III in the new European Gothic style (Henry was said to have had a 'refined mind and cultivated tastes') and dating back originally to the eleventh century, to the reign of Edward the Confessor, canonised in 1161, the last but one of England's Saxon kings. The Abbey had been consecrated on Holy Innocents Day 1065, just a year before the coronation in the Abbey, on Christmas Day 1066, of the victorious William the Conqueror. Since then all but two of England's monarchs, Edward V and Edward VIII, have been crowned in the Abbey, and they only missed out because at the age of 12 poor Edward of York, who reigned for just eight weeks, was deposed and murdered by his uncle Richard III, and Edward VIII had the decency to abdicate. And until Victoria built her gruesome mausoleum in the grounds of Frogmore House at Windsor, and her descendants on the throne opted for

St George's Chapel, a good many monarchs were buried at the Abbey as well. Partly because of its close links with royalty the Abbey has become a place of pilgrimage, for with its royal tombs, its shrine to Edward the Confessor, its memorials to statesmen and poets, its choice of location for the grave of that mysterious soldier the Unknown Warrior, it seems to symbolise the very English idea of a unique relationship between Church and State. Once the duke and duchess of York had decided on a wedding in Westminster Abbey in 1923 rather than a more usual hole-in-the-corner ceremony in one of the Chapels Royal (it was not uncommon for royalty at one time to be married in a secular setting like a drawing room) the Abbey became even more ablaze with pageantry. Four years before Edward's arrival it had witnessed the marriage of Princess Elizabeth and the Duke of Edinburgh..(In *Westminster Abbey*[2] Edward slipped up when he said that Queen Victoria's marriage 'was conducted privately at St George's Chapel, Windsor.' She was married in the Chapel Royal at St James's Palace, and spent her peculiarly hectic three-day honeymoon at Windsor.)

In view of the uncertain temper of relations between some members of the Chapter, Edward must have noted with approval at his first Chapter meeting how, as in cabinet, no personal names were used but everyone was addressed by their title; Mr Dean, Mr Archdeacon. Chapter meetings were held in the Jerusalem Chamber, built at the west end of the Abbey by a fourteenth century abbot, Nicholas Litlyngton. In almost every nook and cranny of the building Edward was hemmed in by the past; it was in the Jerusalem Chamber that in 1413 Henry IV, who had deposed Richard II, died, and here, too, that much work was carried out on the Authorised Version of the Bible.

But of course before Edward could attend a Chapter meeting he had to be installed as a canon, and this he duly was at Festal Evensong on 27 March 1951. The ceremony commenced in the Jerusalem Chamber, where Edward made and subscribed 'the two Declarations required by the Clerical Subscriptions Act, 1865, the Dean attesting the same.' There Edward remained until after the first Lesson, when the Precentor, attended by the Canon's Verger, arrived to conduct him 'into the Church'- 'the collegiate church of St Peter in Westminster, usually called Westminster Abbey.' The Precentor walked on his right side, the Chapter Clerk on his left. On arrival at the Dean's stall the 'Grant and Mandamus' were presented to Alan Don, who handed them back to the Chapter Clerk for him to read. It was then the Precentor's turn to hand Edward a Latin Declaration 'which the canon shall forthwith make.'

That done, the Dean took Edward by the hand to 'lead him to the vacant Stall,' and after 'placing him therein' he said:

Cape hanc sedem, ut Dei gloriam tua authoritate et exempio illustres,
et Corpus Christi in hac Ecclesia aedificandum diligenter cures: quod ut
efficaciter praestes, Spiritus Sancti gratiam tibi largiatur Dominus. Amen.

Following the Creed the Precentor prayed as follows: 'Almighty God, by whose providence thy servant Edward Frederick is constituted Canon of this Collegiate Church, give unto him such a measure of thy grace that what he has here openly promised, and whatsoever his office doth demand, he may most faithfully perform to the praise and glory of thy name and the enlargement of thy Church.'

After the service Edward was conducted by the Dean back to the Jerusalem Chamber and placed 'in a Seat at the Table,' the Dean saying:

Cape hanc item sedem in domo Capitulari, ut fideliter tractes negotia hujus
Ecclesiae Collegiatae cum fratibus tuis Praebendariis as Dei gloriam et
totius Collegii omniumque ejus partium salutarem conservationern; quod ut
efficaciter praestes, Spiritus Sancti gratiam tibi semper largiatur Dominus.
Amen.

In the congregation had been a large contingent from Stanmore, one of whose number reported in the Stanmore Parish Magazine that April, 'There he was, looking very gay and springlike in light overcoat and many coloured muffler, evidence of the desire of the clergy of today to be dressed as far as possible like normal human beings.' We may safely assume Edward had not been installed in mufti, but had gone to the West Door to greet his former parishioners having first disrobed. As a canon of a Royal Peculiar he was now entitled, as are the Sovereign's chaplains, to wear a scarlet cassock. Apparently Edward had read his Declaration 'so slowly and clearly that even your correspondent's rusty Latin enabled him to apprehend that the Declaration included a promise to reside at least four months and four days within the Precincts and to repel any episcopal interference with the rights of a Royal Peculiar.'

Whatever doubts Edward may have entertained about accepting the fifth canonry he was soon to be swept up in the ceremonial life of the Abbey as well as the liturgical. The year of his arrival saw the first service in the Abbey for the Order of the Bath held since before the war. On 24 May, at a ceremony in the Henry VII Chapel, the King installed his brother the duke of Gloucester as Great Master of the Order.[3] Everyone noticed how ill the King looked, and on his return home he retired to bed - officially with influenza. A shadow was discovered on his left lung. 'The doctors are happier about me tonight than they have been for a week,' he bravely told his mother, Queen Mary, on 31 May. By 11 September a portion of tissue had been removed for examination. The King had a malignant growth, brought on by heavy smoking, and his lung was removed. He had been seriously ill in January 1948 with arteriosclerosis, had been forbidden by his doctors to undergo a tour of Australia and New Zealand, and on 12 March 1949 he had undergone a previous operation at Buckingham Palace. By the time he travelled to London Airport on 31 January 1952 to see Princess Elizabeth and the Duke of Edinburgh off to East Africa, and then, hopefully, to Australia and New Zealand to carry out a tour now totally beyond the King's capacity, he looked a stricken man. On the morning of 6 February he was discovered to have died in his sleep.

There was no question of George VI being buried in the Abbey; he had chosen a small side chapel on the north aisle of St George's Chapel, Windsor for his last resting place. But without a doubt the new young sovereign, Elizabeth II, would be crowned in the Abbey, and so extensive were the preparations and rehearsals that for a year before the ceremony, on 2 June 1953, the Abbey had to be closed to visitors. Rehearsals occupied 10 days during May, and after the coronation the Abbey remained out of commission for four months while scaffolding was being dismantled. Coronation year gave Edward some inkling of what lay in store for him by way of fund raising. An appeal for £1 million was launched in order to carry out vital repairs. Any dean who found his repair bill to be a mere £1 million today would sing a Te Deum in gratitude, although £1 million in 1952 was a considerable sum. £10 million was the amount eventually required, much of it garnered while Edward was either Treasurer, as he became in 1959, or dean.

Edward filled some of his spare time now by giving talks on the spiritual significance of the coronation, and a lull in the duties that normally befall a residentiary canon during his period 'in residence' also meant that he could easily accept a request from the Bishop of London to write his 1953 Lent Book.[4] His chosen subject, the life of St Paul, appealed to him enormously. 'It is just because of his concern for people that Paul interests us today,' Edward wrote. 'As we read about him in the Acts of the Apostles, and more especially ponder over the very letters which he wrote, we soon forget that he was a Jew of the first century, living in

an age when modern science was as yet unborn.' Referring to a letter
from Paul to Timothy, and quoting from St Paul's words, 'Do your best to
come to me as soon as you can,' Edward commented, 'We know exactly
what lies behind the anxiety, for it is companionship and friendship which
are the most valuable and stimulating experiences of life. When we are
privileged to have a friendship with a really alive person then we are
thrice blessed.'

Publication elicited a welcome letter from Roger Lloyd, since 1937 a
residentiary canon of Winchester. 'May I congratulate you most warmly
on your Lent book *That Man Paul*,' he wrote. 'I have read it in two gulps
because I found it much too interesting to put down. I think I've read
every one of the Bishop of London's Lent Books, and after Dean Inge's
classic I think yours is easily the best. I did one of them myself and know
how hard this sort of book is to do. Mine cost more trouble than any
of the longer books I've done; and, as one writer to another, I'm left
marvelling how you did it. It's interesting and illuminating. The narrative
flows beautifully and flags nowhere, and the prose style is exactly right at
every point. It must have been a very tricky job because so much of the
narrative has to take place, so to say, in Paul's own mind. But you've so
completely mastered the material that if you did have any difficulty with
it there's not a hint or trace of it now.'

It was little wonder that five days after the coronation, when Lilian
gave birth to her third son, they decided to call him Paul. Unlike her
father's coronation in 1937, when the queen's procession was held up
because a Presbyterian chaplain fainted, the dean nearly got the king to
don a vestment inside out, the archbishop managed to cover up with his
thumb the Coronation Oath the king was trying to read, and the Lord
Chamberlain's hands 'fumbled and shook' so much the king had to fix his
own sword belt (he later told his daughter he would not have employed
him as a valet), Elizabeth's great day, apart from the pouring rain, went
without a hitch. Edward's not too demanding role was to carry the orb,
and afterwards to chronicle the occasion for the library archives, but
it must still have been an exhausting occasion; the Abbey doors were
opened at six in the morning, the Regalia Procession moved through the
cloisters at 9.30am and the Queen was not due to arrive until 11 o'clock,
nor to be crowned before a very precise 12.34pm. Edward and Lilian's
eldest son, David, was one of the youngest members of the congregation.

Edward was beginning to find himself in demand as an after dinner
speaker as well as preacher and lecturer, and so successful was he at
these activities he also found himself being asked to write after dinner
speeches for other people. It would not have occurred to him to refuse,
for he was by nature a generous man, generous, in particular, with the

valuable commodity of time. And even when it might have been quicker to pick up the telephone or wait until he bumped into a neighbour in the cloisters Edward would spare the time to put pen to paper, for in any event, in his early days at Westminster the other members of the Chapter were of a generation for whom letter writing was the normal form of communication. In 1956, for instance, he was writing to Charles Smyth to congratulate him on a publication called *Church and Parish*, Smyth, then in his last year at the Abbey, replying on 6 April on notepaper headed St Margaret's Church. Smyth, in turn, said he was 'much looking forward to your *Henry Compton*,' which he was sure would be an important contribution to learning. Compton was a seventeenth century bishop of London, whose biography Edward in fact called *The Protestant Bishop*.

'Disastrous news about my book "The Protestant Bishop"' Edward had pessimistically noted in his diary on 16 January. 'After having been listed at 18 shillings it is now to be published at 35 shillings [£1.70]. This seems to me to have killed its sale before it begins.' He gave a copy to Smyth, modestly forbearing to autograph it, and was told by Canon Smyth on 7 June, 'This is obviously a great book.' The dedication, "Coniugi dilectissimae cuius cura hoc mea manu scriptum opus si incuriose perdidissem semel et saepius reciperabat" (For my beloved wife, by whose care this work was written by my own hand. If I erred carelessly, she corrected me time and again), Smyth thought charming. 'Of course,' he wrote, 'Latin *is* the only language for that kind of thing!' He added a postscript: 'I hope that somebody sometime will write a companion volume entitled "The Liberal Canon"! (and you can take that any way you like).'

It was only eight years since Edward had published his Life of Thomas Tenison, and in the meanwhile he had written, in collaboration with Dr A Tindal Hart, *The Nineteenth Century Country Parson*. This compilation of anecdotes and diaries had been written by December 1951 although it was not published until 1954, the year that Edward was elected a Fellow of King's College, London. The time lag between writing and publishing, and the fact that it was printed and published by an obscure firm in Shrewsbury, Wilding & Son, would indicate that the book had not been commissioned. And in order to research and write his Life of Henry Compton, a bishop 'almost unknown to the general reader,' as Edward remarked in his Foreword, it had been necessary to consult papers in the Bodleian, Fulham Palace, the Records Office, St Paul's Cathedral, at Winchester and in the British Museum.

In 1955 the Carpenters transferred to No 7 Little Cloister, with a garden where some 400 years previously the monks of the Benedictine Abbey had their oyster bed. David had been sent as a little boy to a very smart

London prep school, Hill House, where Michael followed him, becoming a special chum of Prince Charles, whose chauffeur would sometimes conveniently drop Michael off on his way home to Buckingham Palace. Not wanting to leave home, unlike Michael and Paul, who both joined the Abbey Choir School, David entered Westminster Under School in 1955, when he was eight. He left Westminster shortly before his 18th birthday and went up to Christ Church, Oxford in October 1965. It was somehow appropriate that Edward's first son should have shone not only as the academic star of the family but as an historian; he remained at Christ Church as a research lecturer until 1975, was awarded a D.Phil, and became a Reader, and later Professor in History at his father's old college, King's, London.

Edward's apprenticeship, so to speak, as a residentiary canon saw not only a continuation of his literary activities but a broadening of interests outside immediate Church concerns. The summer of 1955 found him in the USA, but not before, in January, although his doctor 'obviously doesn't think there is much wrong with me', he had been referred to an osteopath. 'I have put on five pounds in weight since my last visit,' he noted in his diary, and added, 'But does it really matter?' David Carpenter has commented, 'Daddy was a hypochondriac, frequently worrying about his health. You could see when he was preoccupied in that way. He would sometimes put on a pair of shorts and go for a run to prove his fitness.'[5]

In 1956 Edward found satisfying scope for any frustration he may have felt at not taking up a teaching post when he was 29; he became chairman of the Frances Mary Buss Foundation, which meant he also became chairman of the Governing body of the Camden School for Girls, now a comprehensive, and chairman also of the Governors of the North London Collegiate School. Both schools had been founded by Frances Mary Buss, a most remarkable woman who became a pioneer in girls' secondary education. Born in 1827, she was still only 22 when the North London Collegiate opened in 1850, having taken up teaching when she was 14.[6]

Recalling the occasion in 1976 when a vote was taken at North London for full independence, Madeline McLauchlin, Head Mistress at the time, has written, 'Never before or since have I seen genuine goodness so powerfully at work.' She was referring to the diplomatic skills by which Edward had managed to reconcile conflicting views among his follow governors. He attended school events whenever he could; on 5 December 1966, for instance, he went to hear the North London Collegiate's performance of *Dido and Aeneas* which he thought 'Delightfully done. Indeed, I put it No 1 among school performances that I have seen.' He went on to record in his diary that it was the third performance to have been given in North London of what in effect is Purcell's only true opera, composed, appropriately enough, for an amateur performance in a girls' school (although there is no evidence that Edward realised this).

A fellow school governor, Professor Frank Cox, remembers Edward as 'a caring and kindly chairman of governors who was a marvellous listener and a very astute and sympathetic decision maker.' At a time when Edward's daughter Louise was at St Hilda's, Oxford Edward invited Professor Cox's daughter, who was thinking of going to St Hilda's, to meet Louise at the deanery. 'Edward opened up the doors of the Abbey to show us around and in we went, each with a glass of wine and a handful of nuts. When I asked Edward what we should do with these somewhat incongruous items he replied that "Holy Writ was silent on this matter." I think that this sums him up very well as someone who balanced the religious and secular sides of his life with consummate skill.'[7]

The Headteacher of the Camden School for Girls, Geoffrey Fellows, told Lilian when Edward died that the school's 'integrity and ethos as an institution owes such a great deal to [Edward's] vision and inspiration.'[8] Edward's association with the North London Collegiate School resulted in a warm friendship with Princess Alice, Duchess of Gloucester, who in 1937 had succeeded her sister-in-law, the Duchess of York, as patron. Edward thought Princess Alice 'one of the most intelligent members of the royal family'. An assiduous supporter, the princess attended many functions at which Edward also was present, retaining her personal interest in the school as late as 1993, by which time she was 91 and supposedly living in retirement. When Edward died, one of the princess's ladies-in-waiting, Mrs Michael Harvey, wrote to Lilian from Kensington Palace to say, 'Her Royal Highness feels very fortunate to have known the Dean and to have been able to appreciate what a truly remarkable and delightful person he was.'

The year 1956 was also to furnish Edward with the first of a series of disappointments he was to experience during his years at Westminster Abbey. With the welcome departure of Charles Smyth, who had fallen out with most of the Chapter and led Westminster School a song and dance, Edward eagerly anticipated succeeding Smyth as Rector of St Margaret's, with the possibility also of being appointed chaplain to the Speaker of the House of Commons. Unfortunately Edward had blotted his copybook by preaching a sermon in the Abbey against capital punishment, 'and such a person,' Edward recorded in his diary, 'would not do in a House of Commons church. So Alan Don gave way out of weakness and against his own inclinations. He felt very self-conscious about it.'

Edward also claimed that Charles Smyth had made life so miserable, indeed almost impossible, for Westminster School that an approach to

George VI, Visitor to the Abbey, had been contemplated, 'to get him removed'. When the vacant canonry, together with St Margaret's, went to the chaplain of Westminster School, Michael Stancliffe, who in 1969 was to be appointed dean of Winchester, Edward became convinced the dean had acted simply to appease the school. About a week after Stancliffe's appointment Edward's retina slipped and he spent 'about two months blacked out in hospital.' In a diary entry looking back on these events he went on to say, 'To redress the balance, Alan Don was in his way a bit of a saint with real sanctity and holiness. He had great natural dignity, was greatly generous and beloved - and possessed the finest speaking voice I have ever heard. People liked him because he used to hang around. He was indeed most clubbable. So far as I was concerned he was uniformly kind; and in the solitary instance when he thoroughly and totally let me down - and I still think this has proved tragic for me though many of my friends think it was a lucky escape - it was in no sense true ill-will nor was it a vote of no confidence, it was simply a matter of sheer weakness. He just couldn't stand up to determined opposition. Perhaps,' he pondered, 'it was his own domestic situation over the years which weakened his will. He was very fond of his wife Muriel, and she of him, but they couldn't live with each other or without each other.' When Alan Don retired, he went to live in apartments at Lambeth Palace while his wife removed to Kensington.

Edward's disappointment over St Margaret's did nothing to diminish his support for radical causes. As a pacifist, he was a natural supporter of the Campaign for Nuclear Disarmament and indeed felt passionately about the issue. He went on many of the Aldermaston marches, although never feeling comfortable holding a banner or joining in the chanting. On one march, he told David with some sympathy a story about his old rector George Saywell. On a peace march before the war, George would always get Edward to walk beside him so that they could engage in conversation about abstruse points of philosophy and theology.

Another and altogether less controversial link Edward made with the world outside Westminster Abbey (although in fact meetings were held in the Jerusalem Chamber) was with the St Anne's Society. In 1958 he became chairman. The Society had been formed during the war by Patrick McLaughlin when he was vicar of St Anne's, Soho, and was run as a centre for Christian discourse, its specific raison d'être being to interpret the Christian faith through the use of poetry, drama and literature. On one occasion T S Eliot was induced to read his *Four Quartets*. Dorothy Sayers was a member, as was Gerard Irvine, vicar of St Anne's, Soho from 1951 to 1953, a literary cleric whose friendship with Edward made through the St Anne's Society resulted in his appointment in 1969 to one of the

Abbey's Anglo-Catholic livings, St Matthew's, Westminster.

But the business of filling livings in the gift of the Abbey did not always go so smoothly. Edward had been anxious to find a suitable position for a parish priest whose wife had been divorced, and suggested the Abbey living of Godmanchester, 'which,' he noted in his diary, 'would have suited him admirably, but the bishop of Ely would not hear of it.' Edward did not pursue the matter for he thought he could not with decency embarrass the wife by arousing a public controversy.

Many cathedrals have on their staff a Canon Theologian, to serve the diocese as much as the cathedral, and the roughly equivalent post at Westminster (with no diocese to serve, of course) is a member of the Chapter with some serious academic pretensions who is called the Lector Theologiae. In 1958 Edward was appointed Lector, a position that suited him down to the ground, for he always believed that the Abbey should continue to be, as it had when a Benedictine monastery, in some sense a seat of learning. His brief, so far as he had one, for the Abbey has no funds for academic research, was to maintain the intellectual life of the community by promoting lectures and study days. It was also understood that he was free to engage in his own scholarship, a task easier said than done as pressures on the time and resources of the Chapter began to pile up.

A rather more unlikely appointment came Edward's way the following year when he became Treasurer - unlikely because one does not really associate Edward Carpenter with any great expertise at finance or administration. But the fact is that almost any member of an abbey or cathedral chapter is going to be asked to cope with tasks they were never ordained to undertake. As things turned out, Edward's initiation into the mysteries of Abbey finance at a placid period in financial affairs generally (there was no inflation; wages and costs were proportionately low; books were easily balanced because future expenditure could easily be forecast) was useful training with which to cope with the unpredictable financial problems that were to beset the Abbey once the fear of terrorism affected tourism and wars in the middle east caused the cost of oil to soar.

Edward's appointment in 1959 as Treasurer coincided with the retirement of the dean, Alan Don. His successor, chosen by the Crown after soundings had been taken by David Stephens, the independent-minded secretary for appointments to the prime minister, Harold Macmillan, was a suave and good-looking bachelor High Churchman of 55, Eric Abbott, who although a graduate of Jesus College, Cambridge, was, like Edward, not the product of a public school. Abbott had been Warden of Lincoln Theological College, later Dean of King's College, London, and eventually Warden of Keble College, Oxford, so that his ministry had been spent almost exclusively as a teacher and pastor in intellectual circles. It has been estimated that at least 1,500 priests and bishops must have passed through his hands. While it cannot be said he was lavish with hospitality towards the canons and their wives, outside the deanery, in the Abbey itself, he created an atmosphere imbued with dignity and spirituality, and laid the foundations of prayer and devotion on which Edward himself was later to build. Edward's complaint against Eric Abbott was of a lack of leadership, but there were times when leadership from the new dean, installed on 30 November 1959, was hard for him to offer, for his health was seldom good and often precarious.

Five

BAKED BEANS ON TOAST

The year 1960 saw the completion of the Carpenters' family with the birth of a daughter, Louise. Her education began at Francis Holland school, but she then continued at one of the schools of which her father was a governor, North London Collegiate. When she complained about the amount of travel involved she was allowed to transfer to Queen's College in Harley Street. Meanwhile Paul, who hid in the lavatory in protest, was eventually persuaded to follow his brothers to Hill House. It was to be another two years after the birth of Louise before they all moved into what Lilian has described as a perfect family house, No 5 Little Cloister, an 18th Century house that survived the war. And Edward continued to widen his horizons. In 1960 he became joint chairman of the London Society of Jews and Christians. He recorded, in his diary on 6 December 1966, 'Took the chair at executive committee of the London Society of Jews and Christians. Afterwards had dinner with Leslie and Dorothy Edgar. Very frank discussion of relations of Jews and Christians, socially and in worship. I feel really at home with them both. There is no barrier here to a deep friendship. Leslie and I are to debate at the Religious Press Club next Thursday.'

It was during one of the Society's meetings that Lilian arrived late, sat at the back and asked one or two penetrating questions. Someone enquired who this strange intruder was. 'Oh,' replied Edward, 'she's just someone who lives in the cloisters.'

Amid considerable controversy about the appointment of its first dean, the consecration of the new Guildford Cathedral was celebrated in 1961 by the inauguration of a series of five Guildford Lectures, inspired by the third assembly of the World Council of Churches, meeting in New Delhi.[1] Of the five lecturers chosen, two, Eric Abbott and Edward Carpenter, came from Westminster Abbey, and an astonishing audience of 5,000 was attracted to the lectures. Edward spoke on Our Anglican Heritage, a subject he had sufficiently mugged up while writing *The Nineteenth Century Parson*. The bishop of Guildford at this time was George Reindorp, and Edward reminded his audience that on the last occasion he had spoken in the diocese he had been both surprised and alarmed to find the diocesan bishop, Henry Montgomery-Campbell, in the chair. Montgomery-Campbell, one of the most amusing and witty bishops of his time, told Edward, 'Don't worry, I shall be sound asleep in five minutes.'

Edward believed strongly that one of the great virtues of the Anglican Church was its comprehensiveness, and he spoke at Guildford as a true eighteenth century Whig when he said, 'I want to suggest to you that this comprehension of the Anglican Church is one of the great heritages into which we enter. I know,' he went on, 'there are many people who are critical of this aspect of the Church of England, people with tidy, with logical, and sometimes I think with rather circumscribed minds. There are people who maybe properly remind us that it can all too easily lead to sloppiness of thought, even to a kind of anarchy in belief. But on the whole I think we ought to be grateful that we live in a community which has not been over anxious to define its doctrine.'

He went on to endorse 'Anglican amateurism.' He hoped he would not be misunderstood when he said it was the genius of Anglicanism 'that its parish priest is a gifted amateur ... We live in an age when we are dominated by experts, and there is a great place for the man who can take a synoptic view, who is preaching one moment, who is counselling the next, who is entering into the pleasures and the strains of social life, who is the friend of a family over the years in a continuing relationship. This is something which Anglicanism provides in its parish priests in a unique way. It is part of our historical inheritance.'

It was in the same year, 1961, that Gollancz published Edward's contribution to their Common Sense series, a highly readable book called *Common Sense About Christian Ethics*, dedicated to his four children 'in spite of whose constant interruptions this book has been written.' There may have been an element of genuine conflict behind this seemingly jocular remark, a reluctant acknowledgement that somehow he had to keep in balance his theological vocation and scholarly aspirations with commitment to a wife and four children. They were now aged between 14 and a few months; hence they were all at a demanding age of some sort or another, the third boy, Paul, causing his father a good deal of grief by his seeming inability to settle to anything. The contrast between Paul's wayward development and that of Edward's eldest son would have been all the more striking because David was so clearly made of the same mettle as his father, even working, as a schoolboy, on Christmas Day, his passion for English and medieval history taking priority over almost everything else. Edward himself could burn the candle at both ends, seeming to require very little sleep, and during the day he found it almost impossible not to be occupied - preferably with a pen in his hand. Hence time for his family had to be snatched away by his children from his attention to clerical duties and his writing. Despite this, he was always available and approachable. The study door was always open and Edward would continue with his work unaffected by any commotion around him.

It may be salutary for readers of a younger generation to recall that Edward Carpenter was writing about Christian ethics at a time when the country still hanged some dozen condemned murderers a year, some of them innocent; the fear of nuclear war overshadowed the lives of everyone; when homosexual acts between consenting adults were punishable by imprisonment. Even when he did not explicitly attempt definitive answers - he was too non-judgemental to do that - it was evident, reading between the lines, what his own views were on major moral issues. For example, on capital punishment:

> Without falling back upon any definite Christian insight, many have asserted that capital punishment is intrinsically immoral, disgustingly squalid and monumentally stupid - immoral in that it inflicts intolerable mental agony without an absolute proved necessity; squalid in that the whole apparatus of the death cell and the hangman is offensive; stupid in that there is something preposterous in assuming that society can get out of any real social problem by killing one of its members.

Far from trying to coerce, the following two quotations are typical of his liberal stance. 'It is dangerous to try to meet every popular demand since the cry for authoritative guidance is not usually healthy or adult: but at least to nourish the hope that something a little more definite might come from the Christian Church is understandable if optimistic.' And: 'It is certainly one of the tasks of a great religion to serve as a guide to conduct, and to help people in their capacities as children and parents, as workers and citizens. People need guidance and suggestion; to be reminded of whatever norms there may be in the moral life. What they do not need, however, is for responsible decisions to be taken out of their hands.'

On 19 March 1962 the Carpenters saw their eldest son David, now in Wren's House at Westminster, confirmed by Launcelot Fleming, since 1959 bishop of Norwich - and David was but one of 36 Westminster boys to kneel before the bishop that day, in stark contrast to the numbers a public school can usually muster for an annual confirmation these days. Fleming had no doubt been invited because he was a close friend, through a shared enthusiasm for polar exploration, of a Westminster housemaster, Denny Brock. The same year, although also prepared to become a member of the Central Religious Advisory Committee serving both the BBC and

ITA, Edward began to forge close links with St John's, Smith Square, the neighbouring church to which, originally, his canon's stall had been attached. The church had had a strange, not to say chequered, history, and was now no longer a consecrated building but in the process of becoming a fine new venue for the broadcasting of lunchtime concerts.

Initially an extraordinary, if not indeed unique, example of English Baroque architecture, St John's was the early eighteenth century work of a little known architect called Thomas Archer. He did some work also at Chatsworth, at St Paul's, Deptford and St Philip's, Birmingham, since 1905 the city's cathedral. St John's was consecrated in 1728 only to be gutted by fire in 1742. It was reopened just three years later, but in 1773 the tower was struck by lightning. Nothing daunted, in 1813 St John's became the first London church to be lit by gas. In 1941 it again fell victim to disaster, this time in the form of incendiary bombs, and for 24 years St John's stood open to the sky. It was in 1962 that the Friends of St John's, Smith Square were called into existence by Lady Parker of Waddington, wife of the Lord Chief Justice, and an architect appointed. By 1969 the crypt was ready for a recital by Joan Sutherland, attended by Princess Margaret, and the newly formed orchestra of St John's, Smith Square gave an inaugural concert in 1973.

Lady Sandford, whose husband the 2nd Lord Sandford was ordained at the age of 38, and who enjoyed a distinguished political career on the Tory benches in the House of Lords, remembers Edward as 'an excellent chairman [of the Friends], bringing humour into prosaic problems, always, of course, to be seen precariously on his bicycle, just a little late...'[2] Another Friend of St John's, the painter Joanna Brendon, has described Edward as 'an affable and easy chairman rather than a masterly one, and much loved for that. I was always amused by his doodles on the agenda - animals, I seem to recall, rather than religious icons. Just when you thought you had lost his concentration he would come up with a very insightful comment, and he had a treasure trove of anecdotes and quotations in that amazing brain.'[3] Although in 1964 The St John's Church, Smith Square Act was passed, freeing the church from the legal effects of consecration, two Eucharists, at which Edward presided, were celebrated every year.

Joanna Brendon's reference to Edward's animal doodles will come as no surprise to The Anglican Society for the Welfare of Animals, established in 1972 with Edward as chairman, following a report *Man in his Living Environment* presented to the Church Assembly (forerunner of the General Synod) in 1970. Once Edward had become dean meetings were held in the deanery. In 1979 Edward convened a working party consisting of biologists, theologians, veterinarians and others concerned with animal welfare to prepare an agreed statement 'on man's relationship with animals which would reflect an ethical approach within a factual context.' The result of their deliberations was the publication in 1980 of *Animals & Ethics*,[4] a pioneering booklet produced before the days when animal welfare had become a popular cause. One member of the working party, a bishop and a theologian, Hugh Montefiore, has written, 'I think it was not merely sensible but also the first attempt to think systematically about the proper treatment of animals.'[5]

Edward's attachment to animals and his refusal to eat them raised a problem in the summer of 1982 when London pigeons began to fly around the Choir during Evensong, sometimes triggering off the burglar and fire alarms. The Surveyor of the Fabric was not too pleased either about the mess they made, and suggested playing a recording of a kestrel to drive them away. At a Chapter meeting Edward said he thought the presence of pigeons would have presented no problem to medieval monks, an observation that backfired somewhat when he was reminded that far from causing a problem, in the Middle Ages the monks would have snared the pigeons and popped them into a pie.

It was generally easy to lure Edward to a service for animals (after he had retired, and when quite frail, he assisted at a service for animals at St James's, Piccadilly), and one can easily sense his disappointment when writing in March 1983 from the deanery to decline an invitation to preach at an animals service near Wimborne: 'My dear Rector, I am afraid you will think it awful of me but I just cannot manage 9th October. It is a Day of Pilgrimage at the Abbey and I really ought to be here. I hope all goes well and I admire the way you consistently support this cause.' The same month occurred one of Edward's most frustrating experiences as dean; it was in connection with a proposed protest in favour of animal rights on the Feast of St Francis - 4 October. The protestors, about 100 of them, were denied permission by the police to march from St Martin-in-the-Fields to the Abbey on the ludicrous grounds that the Law Lords would be sitting that day. So Edward planned to join the protestors in the Abbey precincts, help display placards and distribute leaflets, and then walk over to the House of Commons to hand in a petition. No demonstration can take place within the precincts of the Abbey without the consent of the dean and chapter, and when the vote was split 50-50 Edward declined to use his casting vote, so anxious was he never to impose his will on other people.

Father David Campbell of the Society of St John the Evangelist recalls that Edward 'once preached at our annual festival at St Edward's House [in Great College Street, Westminster] on St Edward's day. However, he had forgotten the day and surprised us all with a brilliant sermon on the subject of animals!'[6] This was entirely typical of the endearing eccentricity towards which Edward was becoming increasingly prone. It was sometimes a matter of acute timing to tear him away from the football results in order to receive a member of the royal family, and then there was no guarantee his cassock would be buttoned up or his cope on straight. As for mending a fuse, he could not even change a light bulb, and Michael remembers how in his study one bulb blew after another until Edward, his eyesight a strain at the best of times, would continue to work by the dim light of a single bulb. When the last bulb blew he remained in the dark, writing on with the aid of a torch, until a helping hand replaced the old bulbs.

It is not often easy for children to relate to an eccentric parent, but this was not a problem with Edward. David remembers with gratitude his father spending hours bowling to him in the garden of 7 Little Cloister, between the ages of nine and 14. 'He was a fine cricketer, footballer and tennis player' he has written. 'He was best as a slow bowler and really could spin the ball a phenomenal amount, both off-breaks and leg-breaks.'[7] Edward played squash as well. But David noticed also how his father disliked spending money, but after paying school fees he probably had very little to spend. 'As a boy, I found our lack of a car, a TV (until the 1960s) and the penny-pinching which meant my cricket pads did not have pukka white leather straps rather humiliating. The absence of a car was not just money, however. [My father] could drive but he had no affinity with things mechanical. Once, when Grandad lent us his Rover for a holiday, I can remember my father peering myopically at the push button starter and then pressing it anxiously as though it was going to set off an explosion.' Edward was in fact addicted to his bicycle, on which he manoeuvred through the London traffic, if not on a wing surely on a prayer.

Edward's almost total lack of interest in food and drink has become legendary within his family. 'Once in Ludlow,' David has recalled, 'Daddy tried to order us a lunch at a pub bar. Barman: "What would you like?" Daddy; "Well, have you got some bread and what have you?" Barman: "Do you mean you would like a Ploughman's?" a question which completely non-plussed Daddy because he had no idea what a Ploughman's was. In a way this unworldliness was odd, because if you were out with him he would never want to go to an expensive restaurant. "Can't you find some workman's dive, Dave?" Left to himself his favourite meal would have been something like baked beans on toast with ketchup, followed by ice cream and chocolate sauce.'[8]

On one memorable occasion Michael Carpenter can recall his father drinking from a bottle of Château Yquem with his scrambled eggs for lunch thinking it was some of Michael's home-made apple wine. Like many clerical eccentrics, catching a train, and more importantly getting on the right one, was for Edward often a matter of pure luck. On his way to present school prizes in October 1966, as he recorded in his diary, 'True to form, we nearly missed the train at Charing Cross. I forgot the name of the station, queued up at the wrong ticket office, but Lilian, with great nerve, placed herself at the head of another queue and we just made it.'

In 1962, to celebrate the tercentenary of the Act of Uniformity and the Book of Common Prayer, SPCK commissioned a collection of essays, *From Uniformity to Unity*. The editors were Dr Geoffrey Nuttall, Lecturer in Church History at New College, London, and Dr Owen Chadwick, Dixie Professor of Ecclesiastical History in the University of Cambridge. The combination of secular and ecclesiastical history in the eighteenth century was very much Edward's field, and he was invited to join a distinguished band of contributors. They included Oliver Tomkins, bishop of Bristol, John Huxtable and Ernest Payne. Edward's chapter, Toleration and Establishment, provided an explanation for how the Anglican philosophy of the eighteenth century Church and State adapted itself to the new concept of toleration. He drew attention to the influence of Locke upon his contemporaries and, we may reasonably infer, on Edward himself, for in many ways Edward was a philosophical scholar in the mould of William Temple. He had of course covered some of the ground in his biographies of Henry Compton and Thomas Tenison, and this essay may well have provided further evidence of Edward's suitability for the cloister rather than the episcopal palace. There has been a vague rumour that Edward was considered in 1963 for the see of Southwell, but there is not a shred of evidence among Archbishop Ramsey's papers at Lambeth Palace. The anonymous author of an excellent obituary of Edward published in the *Daily Telegraph* on 27 August 1998 wrote that Edward's admiration for Archbishop Fisher, whose life Edward wrote, 'was in no way lessened by the discovery of a letter from the Archbishop to the Prime Minister in which he advised that under no circumstances should Canon Edward Carpenter be offered a bishopric since "he is interested in far too many things and ought to become a professor of History".'

What Edward did become in 1963 was archdeacon of Westminster. To some extent this is an anachronistic appointment, dating from monastic times, when an archdeacon of Westminster supervised the pastoral ministry exercised by St Margaret's Church. In modern times this pastoral ministry has developed into care offered by the Abbey to its staff, residents and pensioners, work which Edward took seriously. For example, on 23 December 1966 he recorded in his diary, 'Reg Pullen [the Receiver General, who received a knighthood on his retirement in 1987 and died in 1997] and I set out at 11am for our usual annual peregrination of our Abbey pensioners. First the alms houses - and to No 1, the redoubtable Mrs Collins. Her husband, an old sailor and Queen's almsman, died during the year. She is about 60, attractive still, with a ceaseless flow of talk ... From Mrs Collins to Mrs Dicks, aged about 70 and born in the porter's lodge. Mrs Dicks is a slut and her room always smells. Though I must be fair, not so violently this year. She always, before we shake hands, wipes hers on a wet rag in order, as she explains, to dry them. Mrs Dicks is the kind of Londoner who is rapidly becoming extinct - a Dickensian character ... Then to Mrs Ryan, a pathetic example of decaying gentility who "keeps herself very much to herself." Her husband was a colonel in the Indian Army ... a Roman Catholic, contrary incidentally to the trust deed of the charity ... On to Mr and Mrs Moore, a dear old couple, both over 80. He was in the army about 50 years ... She is very deaf but always courteous, affectionate and welcoming. Such people are the salt of the earth ... Finally to Mrs Rogers, rather weepy as she recalled her husband and showed us a coloured photograph of him with some chrysanthemums...

'From the alms houses - this oasis of nineteenth century England - we went off to find Croft in Walworth. He was out. The street in which he lives is squalid, and the houses in a deplorable condition. I suspect that they are scheduled for demolition, so no one does anything about them ... Our last port of call was to Mr & Mrs Viner in Regency Street - he 87 and pathetic (almost entirely deaf) and she just over 80. Mr Viner used to be employed in the royal stables and they received a telegram from the Queen - prominently displayed on the wall - when they celebrated their golden wedding. She is crippled and cannot get downstairs so threw the keys to us out of the window ... I always feel that these visits are worthwhile in distinction from many things I do, and for me a liberal education. Got on with my one hundred odd personal letters.'

Edward also had a pastoral responsibility for the parishes in the patronage of the Abbey, and within the decade when he was archdeacon he visited all 25 parishes at least once, and although the dean and canons take it in turn to nominate vicars and rectors to their livings, Edward as archdeacon carried out preliminary investigations. Most of the parishes of which the Abbey remains patron are in rural areas where in days gone by the Abbey owned estates; some, like St Bartholomew the Great, the oldest church in the City, are in London.

Edward's appointment as archdeacon coincided with major changes in the Chapter generally. The year 1964 saw the resignation of Adam Fox and the arrival at 1 Little Cloister of Joost de Blank, previously archbishop of Cape Town; he was installed on 25 January 1964. And the previous year the Chapter had been joined by one of the great twentieth century Anglican clerics, Max Warren, whose knowledge at that time of the Anglican Communion was unrivalled; he had worked as a missionary in Northern Nigeria before ordination, and from 1942 to 1963 he had been general secretary of the Church Missionary Society. It is inconceivable that Max Warren could not have had a bishopric for the asking, even conceivably the archbishopric of Canterbury, and it says much for the reputation Westminster Abbey enjoyed for scholarship and relatively quiet repose that an intellectual of Warren's stature should have chosen to end his ministry in its cloisters. He served as sub-dean until 1973. It says much too for the sensibility of those in charge of Crown appointments that a niche like a residentiary canonry at Westminster should have been found for someone like Joost de Blank, still only 55 but very tired after half a dozen stressful years fighting apartheid. He and Edward of course already knew one another from their younger days as clergy in Middlesex.

In 1966 the pastoral role of archdeacon was further expanded when the Chapter set up a weekly chaplaincy to visitors, active or retired parish priests spending a week on duty at the Abbey in order to be available to visitors. The administration of this new service - it still continues today - was undertaken by Edward, who regularly took his chaplains out to lunch. 'You learn a great deal about the Church of England that way,' he told his friend and eventual successor as archdeacon, Canon Anthony Harvey.[9]

When President Kennedy was assassinated in 1963 the new archdeacon was called upon to preach. He stayed up all night to write his sermon, calling to his aide the shades of Edmund Burke and Shelley. 'For myself,' Edward said, 'I must confess that I found his vital energy and sheer zest for life an exhilaration and a perpetual challenge. Its pace, tempo and sparkle were all so delightfully American. His high intelligence, applied with almost clinical precision to social and political problems, his anxiety to surround himself with experts in every field - these have indeed brought a veritable breath of fresh air into areas of human life too often a sitting target for the stuffy, the amateur and the inexpert.' He praised too Kennedy's passion, saying 'it is passion which moves the world, excites and galvanizes ordinary men into purposeful action.'

In 1966 - an especially busy year - Edward contributed a chapter called Church and State in History to a Penguin publication, *The English Church: A New Look*, edited by Leslie Hunter, from 1939 to 1962 a much respected bishop of Sheffield. As a member of the Establishment himself, Edward's comments on the established nature of the Church of England, seemingly an almost permanent subject for debate, are of interest. 'There is no normative relation of Church and State,' he wrote, 'but only better and worse relations within given and particular situations. Excessive formal discussion tends to withdraw either "entity" from its existential condition. One thing is certain: a Church must be as free as it can make itself to fulfil its primary function. For it to acquiesce through weakness, apathy or sheer love of ease in a situation which could be made more favourable to the cause which it exists to serve must always be a grievous sin; and certainly there are occasions when a Church ought to go into the wilderness.

'The Church of England is not, by reason of its establishment, in this situation; and I would hazard the opinion that at present the establishment, on balance, enables it the better to attempt its task of building God's Kingdom.

'In taking this point of view I assume that an established status is not wrong in principle, necessarily distorting the whole process of building God's Kingdom. Many relations of Church and State are possible and have existed: it is the Church's responsibility to make certain that the one which obtains is the best that can be contrived, not in some Utopia, but here and now.'

Edward's own acceptance of his membership of the Establishment was sealed in 1966 (though he would never have thought of it like that) when he applied for membership of the Athenaeum, the most establishment-orientated of all the London clubs. His name was proposed by the dean of St Paul's, W R Matthews, and seconded by Gerald Ellison, since 1954 bishop of Chester. One attraction for Edward was the library, where he became a regular reader. And to the library shelves he became a generous donor. Although according to the librarian, Sarah Dodgson, 'It is not unusual for members not to list their membership in *Who's Who*',[10] Edward's omission of his membership of the Athenaeum is a matter for speculation; perhaps he felt slightly embarrassed about advertising such a blatant association with the Great and the Good.

But of far greater significance was the fact that in 1966 Edward succeeded Leonard Wilson, bishop of Birmingham, as president of the Modern Churchmen's Union (later renamed the Modern Churchpeople's Union), a post he held until 1990, when he then became an honorary vice-president. The MCU dates its inception from 1898 (the year the Churchmen's Union was founded) and so, by an odd coincidence, the Modern Churchpeople's Union celebrated its centenary in the year of Edward's death. There had been some distinguished previous presidents, including Dean Inge of St Paul's. In a paper he called Integrity in Thought and Life, delivered at an MCU conference in the 1960s, Edward demonstrated to perfection, in his opening words, his lightness of touch when dealing with complex theological issues:

I must confess to a slight personal aversion to attending a conference even if it be of MCU during the month of August. True, the English summer kindly comes to our aid and persuades us of the wisdom of seeking protection against wind and weather: 'Linger longer Queen of Tonga, see our cricket in the snow.' Yet in spite of this, August *is* a traditional time for letting Euclid rest and Archimedes pause. Even the poet Milton plaintively indulged in introspection: 'Twere it not better done as others use, to sport with Amaryllis in the shade or with the tangles of Naera's hair.' The answer is, of course, that usually it is far better done; and the world would be a more fulfilled and happy place if more people were so occupied more of the time. Sustained single-minded seriousness - Hitler is a case in point - can end in a terrible aggression against others. I doubt whether John Calvin would have proved an ideal companion for a leisurely hike down the Rhone valley, though his private awareness of the divine foreknowledge might have proved useful at times with the weather. One of the criticisms that might well be made of a great deal of German theology is that there isn't much fun in it: it seems to lack an elemental grace; it impales us on the horns of an arid, antithetical logical dilemma; it uses words like bludgeons; and when we are left exhausted and battered, encourages us with the tremendously satisfying hope that we must live with despair. I always seem to hear, somewhere in the background, the Ride of the Valkyries. Let me hasten to add that I am second to none in my admiration of Tillich; and it would be churlish not to admit that he had helped me in many ways; but too often his work has about it the breath of winter; we enter the twilight of the gods.

His concluding remarks were equally nimble:

May it not be within such a broad context as I have tried fitfully to suggest in this paper that MCU humbly, charitably and reasonably can introduce a distinctive contribution. We, you and I, believe in following whither the argument leads: we believe in treating people with a full respect; we accept that divine treasures are mediated through earthen vessels; we entertain no illusions of infallibity. We are grateful for the past into which we have entered, and do not regret that our lot has been cast in the not unfruitful field of the Church of England. Yet at the same time, *dei gratia*, we are determined to leap over the wall. The pastures outside are teeming with life. We want to get mixed up in them.

By 12 January 1967 Edward was recording in his diary, 'All-day meeting at No 5 [Little Cloister] of standing committee of MCU. Discussed cost of MCU, impetus and the next annual conference, subscription, the future of MCU generally. I do think MCU has a unique opportunity in the next few years if it can measure up to it: stand for a serious liberal scholarship (beyond query) yet be concerned with the practical issues affecting the Church of England. I should, as President, like to do something about this. MCU used to cut ice in the great days of ... Inge, Matthews ... Can we make it do so again? I think it's worth really trying.'

It was due to Edward's personal interest in the World Congress of Faiths that the Modern Churchmen's Union became involved in dialogue with other faiths. Speaking in Westminster Abbey at the unveiling of a memorial stone to Edward on 27 July 2000 Bishop Knapp-Fisher, a former colleague at the Abbey, said, 'He knew that wherever any gleam of truth, goodness or beauty can be discerned, some light is shed on God's nature and activity. Here is the explanation of his keen interest in other religions and his involvement in inter-faith activities.' The World Congress of Faiths was a pioneering movement founded in 1936 by the explorer of Tibet, Sir Francis Younghusband, and Edward had been a relatively early adherent, having been recruited by Lady Ravensdale, a daughter of Lord Curzon and aunt of the novelist Nicholas Mosley, who succeeded to her title in 1966. 'Went in the afternoon to Younghusband House, Norfolk Square, the new headquarters of the World Congress of Faiths' Edward wrote in his diary on 11 January 1956. 'Lady Ravensdale presided at the meeting of the executive committee; colourful, dramatic, gracious and yet intelligent. She certainly knows her charms, how to dress, and smokes innumerable cigarettes. Acquiring this house is a tremendous financial responsibility - and yet a tremendous opportunity.'

Although in 1966 Edward had become president of the MCU, in the same year he did not hesitate to follow Lady Ravensdale as president of the World Congress of Faiths, whose activities were still regarded with deep suspicion by many in the Anglican Church. On 10 December 1966 Edward recorded in his diary a 'multi-faith service of silence' in the Abbey which attracted a protest service outside: 'a semi-flop in spite of quite a lot of publicity.' The service inside the Abbey could not have been conducted in total silence, for Edward wrote of readings from the scriptures which were 'most impressive. The congregation was reverent and thoroughly entered into the spirit of it all. This must have been the first time that anything like this [Jews and Muslims took part] has been attempted at Westminster Abbey. What more appropriate day to inaugurate this than Human Rights Day.' Three years later he was to clash with the archbishop of Canterbury, Michael Ramsey, who in 1969 declined an invitation to speak at a meeting to celebrate, inter alia, the appointment of the Dalai

Lama as a patron. 'I cannot honestly see myself happily taking part in a function of this kind,' Dr Ramsey wrote on 25 October, 'especially when the World Congress of Faiths is the sponsoring body.'

Ramsey was a traditional old-fashioned Biblical theologian, and although he accepted that Christians should show reverence towards other faiths 'he did not believe that "religion" was a banner under which all should unite as if it contained the essence of what is good versus "irreligion" as its opposite.'[11] Ramsey told Edward, 'Not all "religion" is good, and some of the religion under the Hindu banner seems to be very bad indeed.' He was willing to join in a human rights platform but not a 'religious' platform. He felt the World Congress of Faiths ideology was being used by non-Christian religions 'in order to propagate their own belief in a "diffused" view of deity and revelation at the expense of the distinctive Christian belief in particularity.'

In his reply to the archbishop Edward denied that the WCF was trying to create a new eclectic religion. 'Respect for mutual integrity is recognised as the condition of a worthwhile dialogue,' he wrote. 'For myself I am more fully seized of this very particularity since I have come to know more about other faiths.' He told the archbishop the aim of the World Congress of Faiths was to encourage dialogue between 'mainstream' groups, and the purpose of the meeting he had hoped Dr Ramsey would attend was 'that at a time of division and fratricidal strife the great faiths of the world, within their continuing witness in depth, ought to be able to contribute something to the healing of the world's ills.' On 17 November Ramsey did a bit of back-tracking, writing to Edward to say, 'I think it was unfair of me to use the phrase "the Congress of Faiths ideology" and I was using words vaguely and inaccurately. I should perhaps have said "some of the things said from within the World Congress of Faiths."' He then reiterated his main objection about presenting a platform of 'religion' as the way forward for humanity 'as I am not really sure that it is.' And there the difference of opinion between a liberal philosophical historian (Carpenter) and a cautious Biblical scholar (Ramsey) came to rest.

The great event of 1966 was the 900th anniversary of the founding of the Abbey, and on top of all his other commitments Edward's major contribution to the celebrations was to undertake the editorship of *A House of Kings*, advertised as the official history of Westminster Abbey. It was dedicated to the Queen in her role as Visitor, carried a Foreword by Eric Abbott, and was destined to go into two paperback editions and inevitably to supersede Dean Stanley's *Historical Memorials of Westminster Abbey*. As well as supervising the production of this very substantial tome Edward himself wrote some 100 pages on the Restoration and Resettlement. Other contributors included Adam Fox and Michael

Stancliffe. Writing a Preface to the 1980 reprint, by which time he was dean, Edward noted, 'The future of Westminster Abbey must depend upon the fate of Western Europe and here prophecy falters and prediction fails. History, under God, is an open system. The doom watchers may be right, but I have a Christian hunch that they will prove wrong. Right or wrong, however, I would indulge the wish that the future author(s) of another History surveying the period 1965-66 to 2065-66 will be able to testify that even "in the day when Heaven was falling, the hour when earth's foundation fled" the Abbey upheld contemporaries with a Christian hope and inspirited them with a Christian vision.'

Rather than wait for his eventual retirement, to mark the anniversary, pinpointed as St Peter's Day, 29 June, the Queen made Eric Abbott a Knight Commander of the Royal Victorian Order, an order of chivalry in the sovereign's personal gift since it was founded by Queen Victoria in 1896. It is invariably conferred, in one degree or another, on those who have performed some personal service for the sovereign, but those deans and bishops who receive a KCVO are in effect honorary knights for they do not kneel to receive the accolade (a tap on the shoulder with a sword), or otherwise they would be obliged, if need be, to take up arms to defend the sovereign. Hence no cleric so honoured is entitled to the prefix Sir, nor is his wife, if he has one, entitled to be addressed as Lady So and So. Occasionally a KBE is conferred by the prime minister on some distinguished cleric, and the same rules apply; not having received the accolade he does not - or should not - masquerade as a knight, nor his wife as the wife of a knight. Famously, in 1949 the Reverend Robert Hyde was offered a knighthood, chose to receive the accolade, and was obliged by Archbishop Fisher to resign holy orders, although there is no mention of this interesting incident in Edward's Life of Fisher.[12]

Edward was what one can only - and very reluctantly - call an intermittent diarist. Many major events went unrecorded by him, but in 1966, for example, a mosaic of diary entries gives a vivid impression of his hyper-activity. On 14 October he and the Receiver General interviewed five people 'in connection with the post of Clerk of Works,' only one of them, an applicant from Plymouth, seeming to be 'really possible.' Edward said he could see him getting stuck into the work 'in case of need.' One applicant 'appeared with a magnificent briefcase, immaculate suit and cuffs and cufflinks but soon talked himself out of the job. We are,' he added, 'to see three more.'

On 18 October a congregation drawn mainly from the British Association and the Royal Society attended a 'special service for science and technology' at which the poet W H Auden had been invited to preach. 'His delivery,' Edward recorded, 'was very poor and very difficult to hear and he has picked up some ugly Americanisms, but his matter was excellent ...The creeds, he said, must be interpreted like shaggy dog stories ... Frequent quotes from Augustine and Anselm.' On 13 April the following year Auden was writing to Edward from his home in Austria, addressing him as 'Dear Father Carpenter', to say 'Thank you for your letter of March 31st. Of course I shall be delighted to give permission for a reading of poems by me, provided I know what is selected.'

The evening on which Auden preached saw a service held 'for the Knights of the Bath - polite nonsense but quite agreeable nonsense. The Duke of Gloucester, very tottery, was present with the Duchess and the service was held in Henry VII's chapel. Eric dressed himself up in the robes of the Order and thoroughly enjoyed himself. He gave an address, a very correct and formal address, and I read the lesson from Ephesians. The Dean and Chapter entertained these eminent gentlemen afterwards to a supper in school. The Duke of Gloucester was kept happy with a bottle of Vat 69 ... I couldn't help indulging the odd reflection that I found the knights charming though I suspect that I should have found their opinions most off-putting.' Eric Abbott had donned the robes of the Most Honourable Order of the Bath, the third most senior order of chivalry, because by virtue of his office as dean of Westminster he was also dean of the Order. Little did Edward imagine that 14 years later he too would be dressing up in a resplendent crimson cloak with gold tassels.

When Edward died, Sir Conrad Swan, genealogist of the Order of the Bath, recalled in a letter to Lilian, 'As often as not, before a meeting of the Officers of the Order in the Jerusalem Chamber he and I would indulge in a discussion on philosophy. All this, I think, somewhat confused our brother Officers: Generals, Air Chief Marshals & Admirals to a man, & admirable men as well!!!'[13]

19 October: 'Wrote about 20 letters. Max Warren very despairing over our inter-faith service (criticised in Convocation) to be held on December 10th, Declaration of Human Rights Day. Nothing has been done about it, said Max, because the Dean has sat on it. I wrote myself some time ago asking Eric to hand it all over to Max, but nothing has happened. Max thinks that it is now too late to do anything worthily or to give it the necessary thought ... the nave of the Abbey closed in order to lay down blue carpet for the wedding tomorrow which the Queen and royal family are attending. The closure is quite unnecessary. It is unfair to the public and therefore quite disgraceful.'

Edward's diary is littered with complaints about what he saw as Eric Abbot's prelatical attitudes and lack of dynamic leadership. 'Wedding in the Abbey attended by the Queen. Was not present myself. Eric held forth and, I am told, at length.' 'Chapter meeting beginning at 10.30am.

Tremendously long. Went on till 4.30pm. Poor Eric just cannot keep things moving. Lingers lovingly over items on the agenda like a sweetheart reluctant to depart. Is getting worse.' 'Eric's speech was flattering, fluent and facile.'

'*Furious* to see the Armed Forces service for tomorrow which was pushed through the letterbox. Seldom have I seen a more concentrated blasphemy in some four pages. It reflects Eric's basic weakness of character - or is it the defect of his virtues? He has bent over backwards in a quite nauseating way to please the Armed Forces, though in this he grossly miscalculates their mentality. I suspect they have a contempt for the too-accommodating cleric. If ever there was a case for some corporate thinking going into the drawing up of an order of service this was the occasion. But Eric will never do this; prefers - is it insecurity? - to go it alone. I had urged earlier that the service should at least honestly reflect the ambiguities of the contemporary situation. Is it possible to imagine anything more banal or more dishonest than the introduction to the service spoken by the Dean: "We bid you welcome to this church in this our 900th anniversary year and we pray that you and we together may be Christ's faithful soldiers and servants to our lives end, remembering how the apostle Paul wrote to his young friend Timothy, 'No soldier on earth entangleth himself in the affairs of this life; that he please him who enrols him as a soldier.'" This is deplorable stuff quite independent of the wretched doggerel. The quotation from St Paul is almost dishonestly wrenched from its context. Poor lovable Eric, I just can't understand him. I have written a bitter letter of protest but I shan't send it till tomorrow.'

'Celebrated 8am. Ought to have gone to the Remembrance Service at 10.30, particularly as it has been given the new look for which I had agitated, but after the Armed Forces service on Friday I just couldn't face it. So instead I walked over Hampstead Heath with Lilian, Michael [and] Louise.'

15 November: 'Reception in Jerusalem Chamber on behalf of Fight for Sight ... It was all arranged by Norman Ashton who very properly asked Eric to preside - but Eric declined on the grounds that he could only stay at the beginning for a quarter of an hour. Norman then asked me to welcome the press and guests and told E accordingly. I said to Lilian that whatever happened Eric would struggle in at least to welcome the guests and hand over to me. "But he can't do that" Lilian protested. I was right. Just as I was due to bid everyone welcome in swept Eric complete in cassock and promptly took over. Dear Eric, with all thy faults I love thee still.'

'Chapter. Went on from 9.30am to 4.30pm. This excessive length quite unnecessary, but Eric just can't keep it moving.'

'Attended Dean's second Advent lecture ... There were quite a lot at the lecture, with many of Eric's admirers, who hung devotedly on every word. He certainly put it over well.' Among Eric Abbott's admirers was Princess Margaret, who attended his memorial service in 1983. 'He is a very special person' she once told Lilian.

'Eric's concluding lecture: no comment!'

'Westminster Abbey party for Abbey personnel. Very pleasant and friendly with the inevitable Eric oration.'

'Chapter meeting which went on till 2.30pm. Business still unfinished when we called it a day.' Edward was concerned that the role of the precentor, Rennie Simpson, was being steadily eroded. 'But as Max said to me later, Eric just cannot see the point I was making and didn't seem to entertain any sense of responsibility for what had happened.'

An amusing diary entry for 31 October 1966 recalls that in the evening the Abbey Chapter entertained 'the Provost of Southwark and his Chapter.' The Provost was a wildly eccentric, brilliant but sadly unbalanced Canadian by the name of Ernie Southcott, who in 1961 was most unfortunately foisted by the crown on the bishop of Southwark, Mervyn Stockwood. 'I think they enjoyed it very much,' Edward wrote. 'Certainly in the short speech after dinner in the Jerusalem Chamber Ernie Southcott was much more coherent than usual. I even understood most of what he said!' Eric James, who sat next to Edward, was at that time a canon of Southwark, and Edward recorded, 'Eric James used to be a disciple of the Dean but has long ceased to sit at the master's feet.

'There was however at the end of the dinner a little badinage between them. Said the Dean, referring to one of the tapestries in Jerusalem Chamber, "This one depicts a circumcision - a most important theological doctrine." Said Eric James, "There's a divinity that shapes our ends, rough-hew them how we will."[14] The Dean: "Eric, you are naughty!" After dinner went round the Abbey which looked, how shall I express it, just wonderful.'

It would be a gross exaggeration to describe Eric Abbott as one of Edward's bêtes noir; it was simply that his style as dean was not to his taste, and in later years, as Eric Abbott became increasingly frail and had to keep taking time off, Edward rather resented having to run the Abbey for him, especially as he was never appointed sub-dean. 'The Dean's illness has played havoc with my timetables' he complained one day. In Abbott's retirement Edward warmly welcomed him back, and was lavish in invitations to preach at Sunday evening services.

It comes as no surprise to learn that Edward failed to warm to Mervyn Stockwood, in whose diocese he was once invited to give a talk on the theme What Can I Believe? After lunch 'Mervyn Stockwood came in and said a few words - singularly unfortunate and meant to be funny.'

Someone else whose brand of humour failed to entrance Edward was the archdeacon of London, Martin Sullivan, who, at a dinner at the Mansion House, 'tried to be funny; told a succession of stories, one near the knuckle - but the general impression was bad. I wonder,' Edward mused, 'why clergy seem so insecure as to need to ingratiate themselves in this way - much to the layman's disgust?'

Six

AN ENEMY HATH DONE THIS

By the early 1960s, Edward had been at Westminster for over ten years. Although he loved the Abbey, he was beginning to think it was time he moved on. Never one to blow his own trumpet, he was, in his own way, ambitious and had no doubts about his ability to lead. In 1963 an offer came. It was the Deanery of Manchester. Edward was strongly tempted. He travelled to Manchester with David and Michael, went round the cathedral and looked at the Deanery, a large house in the suburbs with its own grounds and tennis court. But in the end he decided not to go. There were several reasons. One was Lilian's health. Although in the event she completely recovered, she had just had a serious operation. Another was the upheaval it would mean for the children, who were unenthusiastic about the move. David remembers standing in the Abbey bookshop with Edward the day after the letter with the offer arrived when Eric Abbott appeared. Edward asked if he could come round to discuss something. Evidently apprised of what was afoot, Eric said 'Oh, has a letter arrived?' To which David blurted out 'Yes, and we don't want to go!' Ultimately, however, the strongest reason for the refusal was Edward's reluctance to leave London where so much of his ministry was based. There was still much to do at the Abbey itself, especially with the 900th anniversary coming up in 1966. And then, if he went to Manchester, he could scarcely be a candidate for the Deanery of St Paul's, which, as Edward knew, was likely to become vacant in the next few years.

On 2 November 1966 Edward Carpenter wrote in his diary, 'Received a letter from Walter Matthews, Dean of St Paul's, telling me of his intention to resign from St Paul's on Ascension Day and saying that he would like me to be his successor.' Dr Matthews had written: 'I don't intend to make the mistake of trying to appoint my successor, but I shall probably be asked my opinion by someone and your name has already been mentioned. I would put you at the top of my list if I had one and I want to know "sub visa" whether you would like to be considered. The job is, of course, wonderful in many respects and I have often wondered what strange providence or chance placed me in it.' But he went on to warn Edward of a number of disadvantages to accepting the deanery. The income, he said, was not enough 'for a family and hospitality in this large house,' and the future of the Deanery itself was in any case problematic; Dean Matthews thought it might be pulled down or even fall down.

Edward received Matthews's letter with mixed emotions. He told the dean, who had been at St Paul's since 1954 and was one of the most distinguished Anglican scholars of his time, that St Paul's was the one Church appointment which would give him the greatest satisfaction to hold. On the other hand, he told his diary, 'Frankly, I cannot see this coming off, in the main because of the hesitancy by authority to put me on a chapter with John Collins [a residentiary canon of St Paul's since 1948] since we have been associated with each other on Christian Action. This is really nonsense - but I can understand the hesitation. JC, for whom I have a great admiration, indeed affection, and know intimately, does not "tick" with Harold Wilson [prime minister since October 1964, hence currently responsible for crown appointments] and is therefore likely to be left at St Paul's as neither the A of C [Michael Ramsey, Archbishop of Canterbury since 1961] or Bishop of London [Robert Stopford, also at London since 1961] will take an initiative to prefer him. Actually, if I were to go to St Paul's I would not meet the same difficulties from John as might others. I have always been frank with him and would never hesitate to stand my ground when need be. J knows this as well ... What I must not do is to build up any excessive hopes otherwise I might land myself in a shattering disappointment, develop a chip on my shoulder and become thoroughly jaundiced. I have seen far too many examples of this happening: but it is easier to talk about this than avoiding it in oneself. Still, if this doesn't come off - and I would not lift a finger myself to make it happen - I shall certainly find myself in a quandary as to what to do. Would I be wise, as I really don't want to leave London, to reconcile myself to staying at the Abbey? If I left London so many of the things I am interested in would have to go by the board ... There must be many contenders for St Paul's, perhaps some who would do it far better than I would, though of course I don't like to admit this. What I do know is that if I am passed over in spite of my philosophy I shall be shattered!!'

On 29 November Edward attended a meeting of the Commission looking into the payment and deployment of the clergy, and during lunch Lord Silsoe, the First Church Estates Commissioner, told Edward that Dick Milford, Master of the Temple since 1958, would be resigning in two years. He asked Edward whether he would like to succeed him - if he did not go to St Paul's. Apparently Edward laughed and said he would much prefer the latter. 'Don't worry,' Silsoe told him, 'it's in the bag!' 'I wonder!!!' was Edward's diary comment. In early January the following year, 1967, the London *Evening News* printed a reference to Edward's possible preferment to St Paul's, which had been read by his father, Dr Matthews having now formally tendered his resignation. Edward explained to his father that newspaper gossip by no means meant the matter was clinched; indeed, that it could easily prejudice his chances. 'I hover,' he admitted in his diary on 15 January, 'between optimism and despair. The fact is that I want to go there too much.' What fortunately Edward did not know was that Canon Collins was hoping too that he would be appointed dean.

21 January: 'Another reference to me apropos St Paul's - this time in the *Telegraph*. An enemy hath done this.'

12 May: 'Today was Walter Matthews's last day as Dean. The *Daily Mail* carried an article showing photographs of six people (myself included) and estimating their chances. The *New Statesman* attempted something a little more refined and affirmed that if Wilson had the courage he would appoint either John Collins or myself!!' Distracting though Edward may have found so much news coverage in 1967, at least in his day the press still took an intelligent interest in Church affairs. It is unlikely in the twenty-first century that any journalist on the news desk of more than a couple of daily newspapers could name the dean of St Paul's.

Invariably when being vetted for the deanery of St George's, Windsor candidates - and there may be as many as four - are put through their paces by being invited to preach at All Saints, the private chapel in the grounds of the Royal Lodge, Windsor Great Park, the Windsor residence of the Queen Mother. And whenever the Queen is in residence at Windsor Castle, shortly before 11 o'clock she drives - or is driven by the Duke of Edinburgh if he is at home - down the Long Walk to join Queen Elizabeth for matins in private at All Saints in preference to being stared at in St George's Chapel. Although he was certainly not being considered for the Windsor deanery - he would have been invited to stay and dine the night before had that been the case - on Trinity Sunday 1967, 21 May, Edward found himself in the pulpit at All Saints. By this time however the appointment of a new dean of St Paul's had almost certainly been ratified by the Queen. But the timing of Edward's visit to Windsor was so close to the crucial appointment to St Paul's to speculate that something we do not know about lay behind it or perhaps it was just an extraordinary coincidence.

Edward preached on the family, 'suggesting it mirrored, when it was a fulfilled family, something of the life of God.' He said the church was 'very villagey', the service 'short and well conducted.' He 'had a chat with the Queen. She told me that she preferred going to the village church rather than St George's, though she tactfully added, "It is better for the children."'

By a stroke of cruel irony, three days later Edward found himself dining with the archdeacon of London. 'Most pleasant evening. Discussed books and English literature, divorce and marriage, inter-faith services etc, etc. What a friendly chap Martin Sullivan is.' In an undated letter to David, written in fact on 26 May, Edward wrote, 'St Paul's as a prospect for me is now rapidly receding.' He had already confided to David, on 19 May, that he had 'more or less given up any hope of St Paul's. I find it difficult not to believe that the person who is going there hasn't had some informal approach by this time. In my heart I always took a pessimistic view of my chances!!'

Whether Edward's pessimism was justified or not, he was in for the major disappointment of his entire ministry. Not only was the deanery of St Paul's, a position of great dignity and prestige at the heart of Church and State affairs, not offered to him, it went to someone so obviously inferior in every conceivable way, the egregious archdeacon of London and residentiary canon of St Paul's, Martin Sullivan.

On 2 June Edward had caught an early train from Charing Cross in order to preach at Benenden, with Princess Anne, a pupil at the school, sitting opposite him in the choir. Typically, he noted in his diary, 'But I didn't recognise her.' He stayed on for 'an excellent lunch' which he had to leave 'before the end to catch the 3.47 to London Bridge. When I got home feeling rather on top of the world Lilian, who was with Betty Mercy and Lady Pickard, said to me, "Have you heard the news?" "No" I replied. "Martin Sullivan is the new Dean of St Paul's."

'I just could not believe it. I was stunned, and my whole universe seemed to collapse around me as hopes secretly entertained for many years (I see now unwisely) were once and for all time shattered. I say hopes, but in my heart of hearts I had always doubted whether such a timid institution as the Church of England would place me at St Paul's so long as John Collins was there. But it had *never* entered my head in my wildest moments that a man so utterly uncultured, slightly vulgar, with really nothing whatever to commend him for the post, could ever - though I knew him to be crudely ambitious - find himself in it ... It is clear to me that the Bishop of London [Dr Stopford], an infinitely little man, would go to any lengths to have even littler men around him.' Whatever the extent of Stopford's involvement, crucially Sullivan was very popular in the City.

Pausing while penning this distressing cri de coeur to exonerate the prime minister's appointments secretary ('It is equally clear that John Hewitt has kept out of this altogether') Edward went on to write, 'I can *honestly* say that if someone of distinction had gone to St Paul's - John Collins or Owen Chadwick - though I should still have been disappointed, my disappointment would have been quite different; and there would have been no sense of outrage.'

John Collins and his wife Diana had invited Edward and Lilian to their house in Amen Court that evening, no doubt to pour out consoling drinks, but Edward recorded, 'I felt I just couldn't face it. But later we asked them round to us, as we had no baby sitter. Meanwhile, the telephone bell rang and rang as friends conveyed commiseration and complete astonishment...

'John and Diana arrived about 9pm. For John this is the most humiliating experience possible. No Bishop of London of any charity or sensibility would contemplate it. To put the most junior canon over the heads of all the others and above a man of such distinction as John is quite intolerable. If it could ever be justified - and I don't think it can - this could only be if Martin Sullivan were a man of such fantastic ability that everyone would see it to be right. As it is, no one would ever think of him in the context of this appointment at all. So John's plight is far worse than mine.

'I have never seen John or Diana in such a state of anger - righteous anger - and upset. John has to say something about MS at the St Paul's dinner, and also install him. I think Lilian and I helped them by licking our own wounds together, by drawing up possible speeches etc. Perhaps gin and whisky helped even more. John really has nothing but contempt for MS - his ambition, his yesmanship. Our session lasted to well gone 1 o'clock. In the course David rang up from Oxford, absolutely furious, bless him ... Michael, on hearing the news, simply said, "If you have any ability don't be a clergyman in the Church of England." I don't think I slept at all when I went to bed. It was a long night.'

Martin Sullivan had been born in Auckland, New Zealand, in 1910. For one year after the war he had served on the staff of St Martin-in-the Fields, had been dean of Christchurch, New Zealand from 1951 to 1962, returning to England in 1962 to become Rector of St Mary's, Bryanston Square for a year. He had been a member of the Chapter of St Paul's since 1963. A number of mysteries surround the appointment of Sullivan and the overlooking of Edward, some of which have achieved the status of mythology. The least surprising event was the publication by Sullivan only a year after his appointment of a book with the facetious title *A Funny Thing Happened to me on the Way to St Paul's*. An almost certainly apocryphal story went the rounds that the Duke of Edinburgh had taken an interest in the matter, saying one day, 'Send for the archdeacon,' and they sent for the wrong one. The biggest mystery of all is why Harold Wilson, who was firmly established as prime minister by 1967, and was to make amends in 1974 at the start of his second spell in office by making Edward dean of Westminster, did not take an active role on his behalf in

1967. After Edward had been appointed to the Westminster deanery he got rather fed up with Wilson saying to him, 'Now you know why I didn't send you to St Paul's. I was saving you for Westminster.' Edward politely pretended to believe him.

Joseph McCulloch, Rector of St Mary-le-Bow in the City, a brief walk from St Paul's Cathedral, believed that Sir Kenneth Grubb, from 1959 to 1970 an influential chairman of the House of Laity of the Church Assembly, had intervened on Sullivan's behalf; and McCulloch sent Edward a brilliant account of events as he envisaged them:

"The Lament of the Ecclesiastically Unpreferred on hearing that the new Dean of St. Paul's owes his appointment to the express recommendation of Sir Kenneth Grubb to the Prime Minister."

> Ah me, ah me, the boots I've licked
> Mistakenly - ah, there's the rub!
> Of all the names I might have ticked
> I never chose Sir Kenneth Grubb.
>
> Of what avail The Athenaeum?
> (I never could afford the sub !)
> I might be singing now Te Deum
> Had I but known Sir Kenneth Grubb.
>
> I could have saved much lucubration
> And got my learning in a pub,
> Had I but realised the nation
> Was mainly run by Kenneth Grubb.
>
> Why did I mingle with the gaiters,
> Endure the dignitaries' hubbub,
> When all the time *personas gratas*
> You pushed along, Sir Kenneth Grubb?
>
> The spreading tree of my preferment
> Shrinks to the stature of a shrub,
> My hope fit only for interment,
> Through ignorance of Kenneth Grubb.
>
> Is it too late? Could I recover
> Momentum in that tedious club?
> Perhaps some member could uncover
> Just who the hell is Kenneth Grubb!

One of many people who wrote to Edward to commiserate (he wrote in his diary 'a shoal of letters began to come in all expressing not only concern for me but simply disgust at the appointment') was one from Walter Matthews himself. He wrote: 'My hope that you will have a place in the Church where you can think and communicate your thoughts is unabated.' 'I am very low and dispirited' Edward noted, but his low spirits rose sufficiently for him to compose a mildly ribald limerick:

The Bishop of London is daft,
If not, it's a matter of graft.
To send to St Paul's
A creeper who crawls
Sure deserves a kick up the aft.

'More and more letters,' Edward reported on 5 June. 'I never suspected how many friends I have!! It doesn't seem possible, but one came - of all people - from Charles Smyth.' Smyth told Edward he was bitterly disappointed, knew no one else with whom he differed so fundamentally on so many matters yet regarded with so much affection and respect, and that he felt Edward had grown 'masterly' in stature 'during these past 10 years.' Smyth was not alone when he told Edward he simply could not understand 'this very strange and singular appointment.' He found Sullivan difficult to envisage 'as a successor of Millman, Church, Inge and Matthews.'

There was at least an amusing postscript to this dismal affair. The senior lay administrator at St Paul's, David Floyd Ewen, told Edward that Martin Sullivan telephoned to ask to see him. When Ewen arrived at the archdeacon's house he was told by Sullivan that in a few days the appointment to the deanery would be announced. 'Do you know who it will be?' Ewen asked. Sullivan then handed a letter to Ewen to read. 'But it doesn't say who the new dean is,' Ewen complained. 'It's me!' Sullivan exclaimed. '"Good God!" cried DFE and dropped the letter on the floor. He told me he was terribly upset and just could not believe it possible. The whole institution had been let down. Later in the morning he rang up MS apologising for what he must have thought his somewhat odd behaviour.'

Sullivan's appointment as dean of St Paul's in fact began a run of pathetic appointments to the Chapter, which became a kind of ecclesiastical rubbish tip for any number of the Church of England's unappealing clerics, the appointment in 1978 of Alan Webster as dean being the outstanding honourable exception. And a further cause of Edward's disappointment in 1967 would have been the fact that half a dozen years after joining the

Chapter at Westminster he had seen the publication of a very handsome book, *A History of St Paul's Cathedral*.[1] Who should have been invited to contribute a substantial portion of the Cathedral's history, covering the years 1485 to 1660, but Edward. His 70 erudite pages of text represented a labour of love. The Reformation, as he called his chapter, saw the destruction in the fire of London of the old St Paul's and the erection by Wren of the magnificent building in which he so longed to work. The characters he wrote about included John Colet, the founder of St Paul's School, and across a double spread was a sumptuous drawing of St Paul's in 1883, shown as it remained for so many years, the worthy episcopal centre of a great city; before, that is, the builders' merchants moved in to destroy the site for ever. The book was first dreamed up in 1946, and its publication in 1957 coincided with Edward's decision to throw in his lot with the Campaign for Nuclear Disarmament, whose leading light was Canon John Collins.

For the past three years Edward had been heavily involved with the Payment and Deployment Commission, set up by the Church Assembly after the eminent sociologist Leslie Paul had produced a report in 1964 recommending a major overhaul of the way in which the clergy were deployed and paid; it suggested, among other radical measures, abolition of the parson's freehold. Canon Fenton Morley, vicar of Leeds, was chairman of the commission and Edward sat on it alongside two other archdeacons, of Loughborough and (as luck would have it) London. Eighteen meetings of the main commission took place in the space of two years, and in addition to attending those, Edward was chairman of a sub-committee specifically looking into the question of tenure of office. The Commission's report, *Partners in Ministry*, one of the most crucial initiatives taken by the Church for many years, was published in 1967 and debated on 6 July that year. It received encouraging support from the archbishop of Canterbury, Michael Ramsey, but was heavily criticised by the bishop of Chester, Gerald Ellison, whose reward for destroying much of the Commission's work was to be translated to London six years later.

Still the workload piled up. In 1967 Edward was invited to chair the Recruitment Committee of what was then called the Central Advisory Council for the Ministry, for two years previously he had written, at the request of the Council, a lucid paperback called *The Service of a Parson*.[2] This followed on from his concern with the Paul Report, and for any man or woman contemplating ordination today Edward's wide-ranging survey of the experience of a vocation remains profitable reading. While Edward had taken on board the basic assertions and assumptions of the Paul Report (Eric James, who sat on the Payment and Deployment Commission with Edward, remembers that his contributions were wise and caring[3]) he still believed passionately in the role of the parish priest at the heart of an episcopal Church. There have been those who have found Edward's outlook unadventurous, his sense of history seeming to overpower awareness of the changes in society and the problems faced by the clergy at the time, indeed, that he was never really in the front line of prophets like John Robinson, the author of *Honest to God* and Bishop of Woolwich. But *The Service of a Parson* remains one of Edward's most accessible books, imbued with historical knowledge, certainly, yet devoid of scholarly allusions, written in fact for the benefit of potential ordinands, theological college students, chaplains and anyone concerned with the recruitment and training of the clergy. Among those to whom the book was dedicated was the rector under whom he had served his first title, George Saywell, and the parishioners of Stanmore, those for whom he first had the cure of souls. Whatever its limitations, *The Service of a Parson* provided transparent evidence of Edward's continuing commitment to a life of priestly duty no matter to what ecclesiastical heights he might one day climb. And he never faltered in his admiration of the parish priest and in his desire to help out whenever he could. The Reverend Oswald Clarke has recalled that Edward 'came every year on one particular Sunday to my church and never failed. When he became Dean I told him that I didn't expect him to continue as I knew how busy he was. But it made no difference. He turned up as usual.'[4]

On 27 May 1968 Edward was invited to lunch with John Hewett, the appointments secretary who had in no way been responsible for the St Paul's fiasco, and was clearly anxious to do something for Edward as soon as he could. And Edward must have been aware before he arrived for the meeting that he was going to be offered preferment of some sort. What Hewitt wanted to know was whether Edward would accept the deanery of Guildford if it was offered - not much of a consolation prize after St Paul's, perhaps, but few places would have been other than York or Canterbury. Edward knew the twentieth century cathedral well and liked it very much. 'I greatly admire the cathedral,' he had written in his diary on 10 December 1966 after attending a wedding there. 'Neo-gothic at its absolute best and without the division of nave and choir which makes so many medieval cathedrals difficult for contemporary deployment. Guildford may prove to weather better than Coventry.' He had lectured at Guildford. On 29 January 1967 he was back at the cathedral for the annual commemoration service of the Gordon's Boys' School. 'Having been told that the boys were bored stiff with General Gordon,' he wrote afterwards, 'I deliberately refrained from referring to him until the end. What a wonderful Cathedral Guildford is. I never cease to rejoice in its proportions.' He added, 'Nan obviously hopes that Clifford will be Dean of Guildford when the present man retires next year. Why not? He would be excellent, particularly with the new university underway.'

He was referring to Clifford Chapman, the sub-dean, who in the event remained in that post until in 1973 he was appointed dean of Exeter. But the pressure was on for Edward to go to Guildford. On 15 June 1968, marking his letter Private, the archbishop of Canterbury wrote from Lambeth Palace in his own hand: 'My dear Edward, I gather that you are likely to have an "approach" about the Deanery of Guildford, and I am sure you will not mind my saying how greatly I hope you will consider this. I believe that the post would give you wonderful scope for your gifts - with the charge of a great house of God and its worship and with the proximity of the university bringing so many chances of Christian influence amongst young people. I cannot think of anyone who could use this opportunity so well as you nor of any post where you might now have a [word illegible] fulfilment of your ministry. I feel that you have probably been at Westminster long enough, and that something really significant for the Church and for your service of many people is now open.

'Forgive me for putting in this way what I feel about it, and if I can be of any help to you about it I am of course at your service. Yours ever, Michael Cantuar.

Ramsey was adept at trying too late to placate people who had been messed about. One wonders why, with the immense weight of his office, he had not bent the ears of the Bishop of London and the prime minister and suggested Edward for St Paul's? But in any case, Ramsey was behind the times. Edward had already decided not to go to Guildford. His reasons were confused, and in his continuing disappointment over St Paul's and the hopes he still cherished of a major preferment (but where to is a mystery unless, which is not very likely, he hoped to become a bishop) he drafted a number of versions of a letter to Eric Abbott, with whom he had naturally discussed the informal offer made to him. David Carpenter has commented: 'Daddy was fundamentally a happy man, but he did go through periods of depression in the 60s and 70s, feeling that he had been at Westminster too long and that he had never been offered anything worthy of his talents. "I live on other people's good news" I can remember him once laughing, after asking me how I was getting on.'[5]

Edward told Eric Abbott he had had two conversations with John Hewitt, nothing had been put on paper and he had therefore been spared a formal offer. He thought it a tragedy he had been left at Westminster for 15 years without anyone discussing his future. Had he gone to Guildford he would have given Guildford his total allegiance and would have been cut off from his metropolitan interests. And he continued to write of his disappointment over St Paul's. It seems very probable that in declining

Guildford, Edward simply did not think Guildford an adequate substitute for St Paul's, and in a way that was a blessing; it would have been disastrous for him to have taken on the deanery of Guildford while still regretting the great prize he had been denied. Like anyone who has been bereaved, whether he realised it himself or not he needed time - and quite a lot of time, for the wound was a deep and painful one - to pull himself together.

To Michael Ramsey, Edward wrote: 'Your Grace, That you should have written to me so near to Lambeth [he meant the 1968 Lambeth Conference, over which Ramsey was preparing to preside for four weeks], when your preoccupations must be tremendous, moved me greatly. May I express to you my gratitude for your interest and concern.' And he went on briefly to enumerate the reasons why, after giving the matter 'much serious and indeed anxious thought', he had decided that Guildford, at this stage of his ministry, 'did not quite offer me the particular scope which I felt I needed.'

Edward Carpenter and Michael Ramsey had quite a lot in common. They both displayed strong streaks of eccentricity, although Ramsey's bizarre conduct was in a league of its own; they were both prone to depression but were fortunate in being able to shake off their feelings of doom quite quickly. The truth of the matter was that Edward was a Londoner, and having made up his mind not to leave he began to count his blessings. He certainly burst into life again as this account of the whole episode, written by his secretary, Christine Zochonis, shows. The last two lines are a reference to Ramsey's habit of 'mislaying' any letters he felt unable to deal with.[6]

> How They Brought The News from Westminster to Lambeth
> I ran to my study with David and C.
> I pondered, he pondered, we pondered all three;
> Ten o'clock said my watch as I picked up my pen,
> And midday was past when I glanced down again.
> Four words on the paper stared up at my face,
> Just the date at the top, and the title "Your Grace"....
>
> With the other two watching I had no escape,
> Word by word, phrase by phrase, my epistle took shape;
> I referred to the archbishop's kindness and care
> In letting me know he'd a Deanery to spare,
> And I thanked him most courteously for the great speed
> With which he had noticed my obvious need.

But by lunch time 'twas clear I had settled my fate,
And had come to the point of declining the bait.
As I said to the Arch. (with no sign of ill-will)
Most regrettably Guildford would *not* fill the bill.
And I heaved a glad sigh as I added my name
At the bottom, where 'Yours *dis*-obediently' came.

All at once David groaned and cried "Dad, it won't do!
I will make some amendments". (This Christine said too).
Though I tried to dissuade them my voice was not heard
- And then Lilian suggested deleting a word!
So the afternoon passed, as with most subtle guile
They reshaped my letter, improving (?) its style.

Then I picked up my mac, let my fountain pen fall,
As I dashed down the staircase and out through the hall;
Clapped my hands, laughed, and sang every hymn that I knew,
As over the grass in the garden I flew;
And I waved my epistle up high in the air
Till, arriving at Lambeth, I posted it there.

Then all I remember is hurrying home,
And lots of my friends calling "Edward, well done!"
And no voice but was praising this letter of mine,
And describing its contents as "splendid" or "fine",
(But I thought of the Arch. as he opened his post
Safely tucking it into a drawer – to get lost).

There was a final footnote to the episode. On 16 July the bishop of Guildford, George Reindorp, wrote to Edward to say, 'A long time ago I was offered a job, thought it right to refuse, and someone else was elected.' (Reindorp's use of the word 'elected' would indicate it was a diocesan bishopric most probably overseas.) The rest of his letter is virtually unreadable, but refers inter alia to the appointment as dean of Tony Bridge (a charismatic and greatly gifted vicar of Christ Church, Lancaster Gate) which meant that John Hewitt had lost no time in finding a suitable replacement for his first choice of Edward.

It was already common knowledge that Edward was carrying much of the workload normally undertaken by the dean, because of Eric Abbott's indifferent health. Writing from Taunton School on 11 February 1968, where he was Headmaster, John Rae, later Head Master of Westminster, asked Edward and Lilian if, in the event of his death and that of his wife

Daphne (they were planning to fly together to Tunisia in April), they would act as guardians to their children; and he ended his letter, 'I imagine Edward is working hard - in fact, running the Abbey.' In May 1967 Edward had told David the dean 'went to a convalescent establishment in Haslemere today. He will be there about two months until he goes on holiday; returning according to present plans in September. I saw him in the Middlesex the other day. There is no question but that he seems much better and I should say on the mend. His trouble has now been diagnosed as a blocked artery which feeds the brain. Fortunately the others have now taken over so that if he preserves his strength it ought to be OK. It would be too dangerous, we are told, to open up the artery. He was quite amusing and very chatty. The number of ladies who have made telephone calls anxiously enquiring after him is nobody's business.' Despite ill health, Eric Abbott was to hang on for another seven years.

Edward kept himself over-stretched at the best of times. Entries like the following could be picked from his diary almost at random:

'Meant to go [out] this evening but just didn't make it. Sorry about this but Lilian persuaded me to stay in for once!' A fortnight later he spent the afternoon researching at Church House - for the book later published as *Cantuar: The Archbishops in their Office*.[7] At 4.45pm that day he attended an executive committee meeting at St John's, Smith Square. Lady Parker pressed him to stay and have something to eat, 'But I couldn't as I had to talk to St Mary's Club at Finchley at 8pm ... Returned at midnight.'

'Worked on the Deployment and Payment Commission and was thus forced to cut Church and State Commission.' One week later, having spoken at lunchtime in a City church, he was agreeing in the afternoon to become a trustee of the Pestalozzi Village. In an undated letter to David at Oxford he wrote, 'Not very much has happened here, though I have travelled about 1,000 miles by British railways during the last week – Canterbury, Heacham [in Norfolk], Cambridge, Upton-on-Severn etc. etc.'

But it was not all work. One evening found Edward and Lilian at the Savoy for a buffet supper followed by a film premier. 'To say that it was crowded is an understatement - it was literally bulging to the seams. Film stars - dozens of them, producers, women with wonderful, indeed grotesque hairdos, Princess Alexandra, all jostled one another even before midnight when dancing began. Lilian and I braved the hazards and surprisingly enough enjoyed it. Returned about 2.30am.'

Some episcopal nuggets are worth recording: '8am Communion in Henry VII's Chapel attended by 30 English Bishops. Entertained them to breakfast afterwards in Jerusalem Chamber. I sat next to Bob Mortimer [Robert Mortimer, for 24 years a High Church bishop of Exeter not averse to a drink or two] and Ronnie Williams of Leicester. I like RW - eminently sane and down to earth. Has just published a short book *What is Right With the Church of England*. Bob M was talkative and friendly. Finds meals on trains too expensive so just goes in the buffet car and has two whiskies and a sandwich. He is the rare phenomenon of the motorist who admits to an accident being his fault!! Still has a scar over his eyebrow and has only just got over the shock of it all ... Dinner in Jerusalem Chamber. Sat next to Wand, former Bishop of London [1945-55]. There is something most attractive in his solidity and ecumenical common sense. Told him that John [?] was asked, "What is the first requirement in an Archbishop?" He replied, "Sanctity." [William Wand had previously been archbishop of Brisbane.] This, said WW, was a typical layman's point of view but a mistake. A modern Archbishop needs to be an administrator and he just cannot avoid this no matter how temperamentally he may find it uncongenial. I suspect that WW doesn't think that Michael Ramsey is really suitable. It is difficult not to agree.'

There are a number of amusing volte-faces in Edward's diary. On 7 December 1966, before Robert Stopford had disgraced himself by giving his blessing to Martin Sullivan's appointment as dean of St Paul's, Edward noted, 'I admire enormously the present Bishop of London. He is not exciting nor is he really much of a leader, but he has monumental commonsense and great integrity. These are considerable advantages.' It is greatly to Edward's credit that in the light of later events he did not doctor this earlier entry. Another diocesan of whom he seems to have approved was the bishop of Worcester. 'Agricultural service in the afternoon. All the Archs present. Mervyn Charles-Edwards the preacher, very rural, very paternal, very pastoral, and he himself looking ruddy and bucolic. I felt that he ought to have been leaning over a fence rather than a pulpit, and perhaps singing *Leaning!* ... Wrote a sermon about Aberfan and providence till 2am.'

As a professional biographer, Edward's propensity for not dating letters fully or at all was a particularly irritating deficiency. On '4 December' he wrote to David - most probably in 1967- to say, 'When you get back [from Oxford, for the Christmas holiday] I really MUST have two or three books from the London Library to enable me to complete the first two or three chapters of my book on the Office of Archbishop. I am beginning the writing now - though I have a great deal of research still to do. I thought these books I wanted would certainly be in the Westminster Abbey Library, and was amazed not to find this was the case.'

On 30 November 1966 Edward was recording in his diary, 'Entertained at Scott's Restaurant by two members of Cassels (sic) in connection with my book "The see of Canterbury."' This may have been the working title

Edward Carpenter and Lilian Wright
at the time of their engagement

The Mothers' Union Coach Party at Stanmore c. 1946
– Edward far left and Lilian front row far left

Lilian and Edward outside the Rectory at Stanmore with Edward's brother, Harry, his parents and David as a baby in 1947

Edward's parents, Fred and Kate Carpenter, at Brighton in 1946

Official photograph of Edward when he was appointed a Canon of Westminster in 1951

The Queen being introduced to the new Canon
by Dean Alan Don c. 1951

The Carpenter family on Leith Hill, Surrey, in 1961

The Carpenter family gathered in the garden of No 5 Little Cloister,
on the occasion of Edward's Installation as Dean of Westminster, May 1974

Mr Dean on his bicycle in Parliament Square

Celebrating His Holiness, The Dalai Lama's 49th birthday in the
Deanery Drawing Room in 1984

Lilian and Edward in the garden of their home in Richmond c. 1996

for the book Cassell had commissioned - and for two members of the staff to have taken Edward out to lunch would indicate that they regarded him as a star author. But it was not until 1971 that under its final title, *Cantuar: The Archbishops in their Office*, Edward's tour de force saw the light of day. This is a book (a revised edition was published in 1988 under the Mowbray imprint) that anyone even remotely interested in ecclesiastical history can read for pleasure or dip into at any point that takes their fancy, for with effortless ease Edward's pen strides across the often turbulent political and social landscape from the arrival in England of Augustine in 597 to Fisher's resignation in January 1961. In 1971 Fisher's successor Michael Ramsey was still in office, and Fisher was still alive. 'The time is not yet,' Edward concluded, 'while he is happily engaged as an assistant priest in rural Dorset, to make a real assessment of the archiepiscopate of Dr Geoffrey Fisher.' Yet in 1971, the year of *Cantuar*'s publication (a book that had taken massive reserves of time and energy over the previous five or six years), Edward was to embark on the longest and the last literary marathon of his life, a major biography of Fisher himself. It was not published until 19 years after Fisher's death and six years after Edward had retired. On and off, it became the extra-parochial task that bore down most heavily on Edward throughout his inevitably strenuous tenure as dean.

Seven

MR DEAN

Cantuar: The Archbishops in their Office was dedicated to Edward Carpenter's 'parents, wife and family, and, in particular, to my daughter Louise in the hope that when she gets older she may read it.' Louise was eleven. David was already a fellow scholar and historian. Michael had attended the Choir School and Westminster and had gone on to Magdalene College, Cambridge where he read Natural Sciences. It was the Carpenters' third son, Paul, 18 years old in 1971, the year that *Cantuar* was published, who had caused his parents a good deal of anxiety. From the hundreds of letters from his father that Paul has preserved, some typed well, some atrociously, some hand-written, one thing is perfectly evident; Edward doted on him. His genuine, almost overwhelming affection and concern for Paul may have been some kind of compensation for whatever it was that Paul appeared to be lacking. It is almost certainly the case that Paul had suffered the misfortune of falling, within the family, into a rather uncomfortable slot. Older than he were two clever brothers, one very clever indeed; younger was the 'baby', an engaging little sister who no doubt came in for a good deal of special attention. It seems reasonable to assume that Paul found the business of competing with his siblings almost impossible to cope with.

What also seems odd and yet commendable is that although - admittedly as a boarder - Paul was at school only round the corner (after attending Hill House he was at Westminster Under School and the Abbey Choir School) his parents wrote frequently, Edward at least once a week, and Paul would send home what he called his Sunday Letter. Like those of most little boys, his letters were usually brief, to the point and full of misspellings. Apart from a couple of truly infantile efforts - one read, 'Dear Daddy, I am send the sixpence back which you gave me at Lyions because I am not aloud it' - they have the great merit of being dated. His father's seldom were, and it is only from internal evidence, when there is any, that it is possible to date the majority of Edward's epistles even approximately.

'I hope you are well and having a nice time' another early note from Paul began. 'Why haven't you written me a letter today. I want you to send me a letter every day. Please could you send me som selotape and my football boots. I haven't got a bleu shirt only under school ones they wont do ask Michael he will tell you. Lots of love, Paul.' Michael had passed through the Choir School at Westminster four years ahead of Paul, who later on took to signing himself to his parents 'Paul Carpenter.' He became grander still when he was grown up, calling himself 'P J Arscott Carpenter.'

Paul had a very precise mind. On 19 October 1962, when he was 10, he wrote, 'I would like on Saturday not to have a big tea but to have a big super, with soup if possible starting at about 6 "o" clock.' Five months later, and still far from literate: 'Thank-you very much for the nice pen you sent me this is the writing it writes it's nice isn't it?'

A Sunday Letter dated 30 January 1965 began, 'We have know started work.' There followed a catalogue of demands: for his jym shoes; an appointment for reading glasses ('the type of glasses I want are the Italian type, plastic lenses'); 'some type-writing paper, and some envelopes like this letter was in;' whitener for his gym shoes 'in a tupe if possible'. On 21 November that year Paul confessed, 'I am not getting on very well. I came bottom in form.' But by 23 May 1965, which he duly noted was Rogation Sunday, he was able to announce that he had played 'tennes' with Michael and was now in the 1st Eleven. 'This week,' he added, 'I came 6th in form but will try harder this weak.' He wanted to know what day and month it was in Australia, for his parents were staying at the home of the archbishop of Melbourne while Edward delivered a series of lectures.

A Sunday Letter written on 5 December 1965 began, 'I am sorry I did not write on Wednesday, but I forgot all about it.' Paul was an engagingly frank and honest boy, if a slow learner and naive, and these were perhaps the qualities, along with the handicaps, that so endeared him to Edward. He ended this letter, 'The next match is St Pauls. Again I came bottom of the form.' Sixteen kisses followed.

Two letters from Michael to Paul have survived, one written on Paul's seventh birthday, when Michael was a 12-year-old pupil at the Choir School. 'HAPPY BIRTHDAY!!!!!!!!' he began, with one exclamation mark too many if they were intended to denote Paul's age, and then went on to say, 'I am afraid I haven't got anything for your birthday now for I haven't had a chance to buy you anything, but I am, with any luck, going shopping tomorrow. Is there anything you specially want. If so tell me TONIGHT, slip a note round. The first exeat is on Saturday week, tell Mummy and Daddy, I expect they have forgotten.'

What worried Edward was that others might overlook Paul. 'Last Friday was Paul's birthday,' Edward was obliged to remind David on 10 June 1968. ' *Please* bring a present for him.' When it came to letter writing, David seems to have been somewhat dilatory; Edward's letters to him contained a number of admonitions like 'Do write a letter to granddad some time. Letters mean a great deal to him', and 'Just a reminder that it is M's birthday on Sunday. Please don't forget it.' 'By the way,' Edward wrote to David on one occasion, 'what happened about Giles [Pickard]? He was very disappointed not to see you! ... a little letter of regrets wouldn't do any harm.'

On 3 December 1961 the Master of the Under School, Pat Campbell, wrote to Edward to say that one of the mistresses 'was rather concerned about Paul, about his slow progress and his unwillingness to co-operate with her...

'I had a talk with him myself. He told me that everything was all right, ie that he was happy at school, and that he would try harder. But afterwards he told her that everything was not all right, & he wished he had told me so. He also told her apparently that I had beaten him, she thought he was afraid I was going to. In fact there was never any thought of my doing so, I can't think I should ever beat a boy like Paul [he was not yet eight!], he doesn't need it, it would be bad for him. There are very few boys that I do beat...

'I really have no idea what is the matter, why he should be disobedient, resentful, unwilling to try & learn.' But he added to this somewhat disjointed and pointless letter, 'I am not seriously worried. I feel confident everything will be all right, but I want to put things right for him quickly ... Don't worry about this, or think that we are. Paul is a boy of character; and intelligence too, I am sure. I certainly like him.'

On 11 April the following year Campbell wrote to Edward, 'I hope I am right in my estimate of Paul, as written on his report. In work he is not doing well, not so well as David at the same age, but I am sure he is intelligent & that he wants to do well, so I think it can only be a matter of time. I think he is friendly, more friendly than D was at first.' Paul's attitude towards school seems to have been rather a matter of swings and roundabouts. On 28 December 1966 Edward wrote in his diary, 'Paul came home from the choir school today. Seems *very* happy.' But of course he may have been happy to be home and away from school. It was certainly a different story on 18 January 1967. 'Paul went back to school today. Such a pity that he developed a huff yesterday evening and locked himself in his bedroom. All because Lilian asked him to have his hair cut - as requested by the Choir School.'

Lilian's approach to the problems that beset Paul was of the stiff upper lip variety. 'WORK WELL, PLAY WELL. *Never give up*' was how she ended one letter. Another began, 'Don't lose heart. Be *OPTIMISTIC*.'

Another maternal missive concluded, 'Don't GIVE UP TRYING. Be diligent, patient and relaxed. *Break down the inner wall of partition.* All *is* possible.'

As far as Edward's letters to Paul were concerned (and how Edward made the time to keep up correspondence with all three of his sons is one of the minor miracles of his busy life), as often as not (and even on his 26th birthday) they began Darling Paul. And even when the salutation was merely My dear Paul the letter might end with a dozen kisses. They also almost invariably ended with a drawing of The Saint, a popular television series at the time, and practical encouragement abounded. 'You are rapidly improving' he remarked with regard to Paul's skills as a photographer. 'Thank you for your letters which I read over the telephone to mummy at Margate. You wrote them very well and they are most amusing ... We do miss you.' '*All mummy and I wish to do is what is best for you.*' 'I tried to catch a glimpse of you this morning but in vain. Congratulations on coming out 1st in Latin.' 'I am writing this as I dash off to Luton ... You sound very cheerful. I do hope it continues.' 'Though you have not had much practice your tennis has improved wonderfully, and some of your backhand volleys are first class. We really must arrange some lessons for you as I think you may become a first class player.' Edward was himself a good tennis player, unfortunately injuring his knee while playing in 1966, which necessitated visits to an osteopath.

There was plenty of family news as well. 'Louise made a bright remark today. I said to her (she had bare feet at the time), "If you run about like that you will catch a cold." And she said, "No I won't because I've already got one." That was pretty cute wasn't it. Must dash and catch my train...' 'David rang up yesterday but I wasn't here. He always reverses the charges. I think I know why don't you.' 'I hope you get this letter before you go to bed tonight. I would have sent it earlier but I have a terribly bad cold and have been sick ... Louise had a young school friend to tea yesterday. When I came into the room the little girl said to me: "This hasn't got anything to do with you." Louise said to her: "That's rude. Don't speak to my daddy like that."' 'Must dash. Though I hear some ghastly Searcher record in the background!!! All my love, Daddy.'

'This letter comes with all my love,' Paul was assured one day. 'Well, darling, I must close now; but I will bring this letter round to the choir school so that you can get it this evening,' was a typical signing off. Even with only 24 hours to go before Paul was due to start a school holiday Edward would write to him, ending his letter, 'Well darling, all my love. We are much looking forward to seeing you tomorrow - and your coming home.'

Paul never made it into Westminster Upper School, moving on instead to the Central Tutorial School for Young Musicians (he played the violin). 'Since leaving school without any qualifications I have had a variety of jobs' he candidly informed a potential employer when he was 28. He had worked as a receptionist at the Naval and Military Club and as a security guard, in the wine department of the Army and Navy Stores and as a 'junior outside clerk' for a firm of West End solicitors. But despite such an unsettled career nothing could dim Edward's affection for the son who seemed most in need of him. 'Darling Paul, Many, many happy returns of the day!' he wrote from the deanery on Paul's 26th birthday. 'I can't but think backwards on this day to the Coronation Year and that great event of the year. And then you came, much to our delight. You and mummy soon went down to Westminster Hospital, but everything proved OK. Indeed I carried you out of the Hospital. And so your pilgrimage began. What a lot has happened in between that time and now.' He enumerated Paul's various modes of employment and went on, 'I do hope you can see some sort of pattern emerging for us all in spite of set backs and disappointments ... So,' he ended, 'ALL MY LOVE for a very happy and blessed BIRTHDAY.' There followed no fewer than 19 kisses. Three years later Edward's card read, 'Darling Paul, I wish you every blessing and great happiness on your birthday - and in the years to come. You have brought with you a unique contribution to the family and its life: and as you *must* know I have for you a great and continuing affection.'

About Edward's great and continuing affection for his own parents his diary leaves us in no doubt. 27 November 1966: 'My birthday. Celebrated at 8am. I always remember how Mummy's last birthday card came to me the day after her death. I was giving the prizes at Perkins School, Chertsey - she was very anxious for me to wear a clerical collar - and called on her in the evening. She gave me a meal; but took me aside in the kitchen and said she didn't feel that she was of much use to anyone!! I replied that this just was not true but that we loved having her with us. She kissed me goodbye, wrote out her shopping list, sat up late talking with Dad and sipping a glass of port wine. She "passed over" during the night. To her and Dad I owe almost everything. I am longing to see her again. What a wonderful little person she was, devoted to her family and her church ... Whenever I left Velvines before an exam - I usually got home to swot them - she always threw a pair of old shoes after me for luck. It certainly worked. Dad rang me up this evening. I was so glad.' (Edward's mother died on 25 November 1960; his father on 8 June 1969.) 1 January 1967: 'Went home with Michael to see Daddy. Had lunch with him ... Took Daddy afterwards over Chobham Common to Windlesham and back to Velvines. It was Mummy's favourite ride and I could almost see her with us. What a pleasure she took in simple delights - flowers, a lovely day, meeting a friend, buying something in a shop ... Never a day passes but I recall her with affection - and infinite gratitude.'

When in 1971 the defunct Byron Society was re-founded Edward was asked to join. He became a vice-president, a position he held until his death, and once he had become dean he threw open the Deanery for Society meetings. His fellow vice-presidents included such literary buffs as the historian Lord Briggs, the MP Michael Foot, Patrick Leigh Fermor, Lady Longford and John Julius Norwich. His association with the Byron Society was something of a perfectly justified self-indulgence; his appointment as a vice-president of the Royal Over-Seas League in 1974, on the other hand, he saw as one more opportunity to benefit other people. He assiduously attended the League's arts and music events designed to facilitate the careers of young performers and artists from the Commonwealth.

Despite poor health, by 1974 Eric Abbott had totted up 15 years as dean, and in February, aged 68, he sent in his resignation. By this time, also, Edward had been a member of the Chapter for 23 years. There was not a lot about the Abbey he did not know; his credentials as a scholar were impeccable; he was 63. It was unlikely, having turned down the deanery of Guildford, he would at his age be offered preferment outside London. But the question was, would he be chosen for Westminster? He and the family bit their nails while the customary processes of consultation took place. A final decision rested with the prime minister, Harold Wilson, whose task it was to send a name to the Queen for her approval. A definite glimmer of hope lay in the fact that the Conservative prime minister, Edward Heath, had lost patience with the coal miners' strikes, had put the country on a three-day working week and had eventually called an election 14 months earlier than he need have done on the issue of who runs Britain, the coalminers or the government. On 3 March 1974 the country returned its verdict; whoever was to be in charge in future it was not to be Ted Heath and the Conservative Party. Heath lost the election and on 4 March Harold Wilson returned to 10 Downing Street as prime minister. We can be as sure as it is possible to be that had Ted Heath won the 1974 election, or not gone to the country that year, he would not have recommended to the crown an avowed socialist as dean of Westminster, and although Harold Wilson deserves ultimate credit for the decision to select Edward, indirectly he had the striking miners to thank for his good fortune.

The timing of Eric Abbott's resignation was very strange; a general election campaign was under way, and although it is true that during an election the government of the country continues on a day to day basis, no prime minister fighting for his and his party's political life would be likely to give much time or thought to crown appointments. But that would not of course have prevented the appointments secretary taking soundings, and on 16 April, within six weeks of entering office, Harold Wilson wrote to Edward:

> My dear Archdeacon, It is my duty to recommend to The Queen the name of a successor to Dr Eric Abbott as Dean of Westminster.
> I have given this important question much careful consideration. It would give me very great pleasure to submit your name to Her Majesty for this appointment if this course is acceptable to you.
> I must ask you to treat this proposal in confidence. It is my hope that you will allow me to submit your name to The Queen for this appointment.

Edward lost no time in unctuous prayer or consultation. Although he said he was surprised to be offered the deanery, on the same day that he received the letter, 17 April, he accepted, almost as though he was terrified some wicked witch might snatch the prize from his grasp. Indeed, no ecclesiastical appointment of importance can ever have been accepted with such alacrity.

> My dear Prime Minister, Thank you for your letter of 16 April intimating your wish to submit my name to Her Majesty for the Deanery of Westminster in succession to Dr Eric Abbot.
> I am deeply conscious of the honour you have paid me, and the significance of the office. In accepting your invitation may I say that I shall do all in my power to deserve the trust which you have placed in me.

Among those who sent congratulations was Douglas Guest, organist and master of the choristers, who dispatched a telegram from Cape Town: 'Thrilled to bits.' The news was released officially on 24 April, a select list of 15 clerical worthies having been notified in advance, including of course other members of the Chapter, who by this time included David Edwards[1], the publisher in 1963 of *Honest to God*, and John Baker, who in 1982 was to be consecrated bishop of Salisbury. John Baker had met his future wife, Jill, when he went to work at the Abbey in 1973, and it was in 1974 that they became engaged. When they told Edward of their wedding plans he said, 'That's the best news I've had for months.' Bishop Baker has commented, 'Considering that it was only a short time since he had been appointed and installed as Dean, I reckon that says something about the priority of friendships in his enthusiasms.'[2]

Edward's installation as Dean of the collegiate church of St Peter in Westminster took place on Ascension Day, 23 May 1974. As the text for his sermon he chose 'Why stand ye gazing up into Heaven?' and he managed to quote Francis Bacon, Shelley and Albert Schweitzer. He also estimated the 'Abbey family' for which he was now responsible to number about 100, and claimed also – which was way off beam - that six million visitors entered the Abbey every year; the figure two years later, according to Trevor Beeson's diaries, was only between 1.5 and 2 million.[3] What is an undeniable fact is that the year Edward took over as dean saw an oil crisis that led to rampant inflation, 'which eventually destabilized the finances of many hitherto secure institutions - including Westminster Abbey.'[4] Within a year the Abbey had sustained a loss of £61,000 on the general income and expenditure account, and within two years reserves had been depleted by over £100,000. Beeson, who arrived as a residentiary canon in April 1976, reckoned the annual running costs at that time to be about £520,000, of which £325,000 went on salaries and pensions. The cost of music was running at about £100,000 a year, all of which made a constant flow of visitors essential; in 1975 they provided an income of £216,000, excluding a profit of £47,600 from the Bookshop. But one delightful prospect for Edward and Lilian was of a final move, into the fourteenth century deanery, spacious and gracious. It was a house in which they both revelled, despite the cost of running it and the lack of staff. But just in case of any lingering spooks, they had John Baker bless it.

All self-governing bodies like abbeys and diocesan cathedrals have their liturgical life governed by statutes, in the case of pre-Reformation foundations often by anachronistic ones that hamper development and freedom of action. As dean, Edward now, for example, found that he could only preach at Matins and Evensong on Christmas Day, Easter Sunday and Whitsunday unless invited by a canon in residence. Just a month after his arrival, Trevor Beeson, whose diaries paint a fascinating picture of life at the Abbey for the next 11 years, was writing that Edward was, he supposed, 'the most erudite leader of the community since the time of Armitage Robinson [Joseph Armitage Robinson, dean from 1902 until 1911, when he became dean of Wells, having been appointed a canon of Westminster in 1899]. He is one of the last of the liberal modernist churchmen who flourished for a time in the 1930s. His knowledge and love of the Abbey is unrivalled and he combines the eccentricity of a scholar with a warm humanity.'

The description of Edward as an eccentric has been challenged by, among others, Bishop Edward Knapp-Fisher, on the grounds that he was not egocentric, but you do not need to be egocentric to be eccentric.[5]

Beeson's appointment to the Abbey was partly due to Edward's personal intervention. Robert Runcie, in whose diocese of St Albans Beeson had been a parish priest, had been anxious to find him a post in which, hopefully, he would have more time to write, and had sounded out Edward, who, although he had only once met Beeson, asked Harold Wilson to appoint him to Westminster.[6] Although in the event other major duties - he became Rector of St Margaret's and chaplain to the Speaker of the House of Commons - curtailed his writing, Beeson remained indebted to Edward for his intervention, and had no hesitation in dedicating his Westminster diaries 'with gratitude and affection' to 'A godly and erudite Canon and Dean of Westminster.'

But it was especially to Edward's humility that Bishop Knapp-Fisher, a residentiary canon at the Abbey from 1975-87 (he became sub-dean and archdeacon), spoke at the dedication of a memorial stone to Edward on 27 July 2000. This particular virtue was often displayed at meetings of the Chapter, now far less drawn out than they had been under Eric Abbott; although as dean Edward had a vote, he was always reluctant to use it as a casting vote if there was the slightest chance of the Chapter coming to an agreed mind, or at least to a majority decision. Many times he undertook to reprimand some indolent servant of the Abbey, only to do so in such gentle terms and kindly manner that the wretched offender went away imagining that Edward had been congratulating him on his excellent work.

And of course as dean Edward now found himself on the frontiers of administration, a task no dean or bishop can wholly avoid however ill cut out. Looking back on his appointment as Precentor and Sacrist in 1974 (he was the first person to hold the two offices jointly, the Precentor being head of the Choral Foundation, the Sacrist being in charge of ceremonial) Roger Job has recalled that 'already the great pastoral heart is emerging in his concern that we [he and his wife Rose] should be happy at the Abbey. [Edward] wasn't priestly in any anglo-catholic sense, indeed, he made a muddle on any altar at which he was celebrating. He was priestly in his dealings with people, in his determination to endure all things in his relations with them. For him the supporting text was not so much St Paul as - you've guessed - the Shelley passage which Lilian read at his funeral, especially the bit "To hope till Hope creates from its own wreck the thing it contemplates."'[7] Roger Job recalls that once at Evensong Edward wore two hoods. 'He was a genuine eccentric,' he says. 'There was no element of affectation or exhibitionism.'

Edward found himself, six weeks before his installation, writing to Roger Job to offer him the post of Precentor on the departure of Rennie Simpson, with the prospect of becoming Sacrist too when the acting

Sacrist left at the end of July. In all, at least three letters went out from Edward, two from the Receiver General, Reg Pullen, and two draft contracts. It is interesting to note the stipend of the Precentor in 1974 was £2,000 a year, in addition to free accommodation, and Roger Job was paid an additional £500 a year as Sacrist. A suffragan bishop at about this time was on £3,000.

In an amusing and instructive note to the author, dated 14 June 2000, Roger Job has written: 'By the time I arrived Reg Pullen was the Grand Vizier. He had already worked in the Chapter Office over 25 years by 1974. Reg had everything under control. His great competence and his friendship with Edward were the key to his rise - and the fact that when Edward was Canon Treasurer [Reg Pullen] did the work. Today he would (rightly) be called a control freak. He was even instrumental in having one of the Matins canticles dropped on Christmas Day, and a popular hymn substituted.' Roger Job moved on, in 1979, to be Canon Precentor at Winchester, having been described by someone as the best counter tenor he had ever heard at Magdalen. At Winchester he was to serve under Trevor Beeson when he became dean, and Beeson agrees that Pullen 'was a key figure at Westminster Abbey, and not least during Edward's time when strong administrative assistance was vital. The problem was, of course, determining who was actually running the Abbey, and very little happened without Reg Pullen's approval.'[8] He worked at the Abbey for 40 years and was Receiver General for 28 years, helped organise three royal weddings and at very short notice the funeral, in 1979, of Earl Mountbatten.

An ex-officio office Edward automatically assumed on becoming dean was chairman of the governors of Westminster School, an ancient and somewhat idiosyncratic establishment founded in 1560 by Queen Elizabeth. It was fortunate that Edward already knew the current Head Master, John Rae, appointed in 1970; Edward had encouraged Dr Rae to apply for the post, and having met Rae when he was teaching at Harrow he had supplied him with a reference for his first headmastership, at Taunton. As Dr Rae and his wife were both mavericks, and the school was so closely linked to the Abbey, it was as well that Edward continued to support them. Situated as it is in the heart of London, with all the temptations to explore pubs and Soho sex shops which such a situation inevitably supplies, Westminster remains one of the most difficult public schools to run; its pupils are also so physically tied in to the Abbey premises that unregulated noise, school paraphernalia thoughtlessly chucked down in the cloisters, even banana peel thrown out of windows can dissipate goodwill on the Abbey side, while complaints from the Abbey about unauthorised use of the Green in Dean's Yard can irritate the school. In 1977 Trevor Beeson confiscated a football. 'The Head Master, with breathtaking but unsurprising arrogance, has unilaterally declared void the 1959 agreement between the Abbey and the School,' he recorded. The Chapter asked Beeson, if possible, to reach an amicable solution with Dr Rae, to avoid the matter being raised officially with the School's Governing Body; 'if possible this must be avoided, because matters of this sort are remembered for centuries at Westminster.'⁹

In his autobiography, John Rae admits to some degree of mayhem but shows scant sympathy for what he saw as stuffy intransigence. 'In my relations with the governing body [of the school],' he has written, 'I came to rely more and more on my friendship with Edward Carpenter. Westminster was one of the few public schools whose chairman of governors lived on the spot. The Deanery was a hundred yards from the headmaster's house and overlooked College Hall courtyard where the pupils gathered before their meals. If Edward Carpenter had been so minded he could have complained daily about the boys and girls who flung their books and cases at his door when they were late for lunch. But he was one of the few members of the Abbey community who seemed positively to enjoy living next door to six hundred adolescents. The other Abbey clergy and their wives found the proximity of so much youthful energy a strain on their somewhat limited reserves of Christian charity.'¹⁰

Happily, on 9 June Beeson was able to report: 'Peace has broken out over the use of the Green.' The previous year, 1976, all Edward's tact and patience in dealing with his fellow school governors were required when for a time John and Daphne Rae separated; a divorce would almost certainly have led to Rae's resignation. As it was, John Rae says that when Daphne returned 'one or two members of the Abbey community declined to talk to her.' In 1985 Daphne Rae published a book, *A World Apart*, and then there was a great rumpus, for she had drawn attention to the not very surprising existence of homosexuality at Westminster. It was hardly a novel discovery, but by this time Dr Rae had plenty of enemies on the board of governors, it was unusual for a headmaster's wife to go public, and they saw this as an excuse, together with his opposition (in which he was joined by Edward) to Westminster entering the Assisted Places Scheme, to get rid of him. Having collected a bottle of whisky and two glasses from the deanery dining room, and having repaired to his study, Edward was able to tell Rae he was not to be sacked, merely advised to look around for another job. Even without access to the minutes of the governors meeting over which Edward had presided, it is not difficult to imagine him managing to persuade a sufficient, albeit small, minority to vote the way they did.

On Edward's retirement, John Rae said he doubted whether there had ever been in the history of Westminster a dean who took a greater interest in the school's life. He recalled especially how 'in recent years he spoke eloquently not least to the school at Latin Prayers on the dangers of the new fundamentalism which he saw as the principal threat to rational thought.'[11]

Westminster School was not the only educational establishment with which Edward was intimately connected to experience problems. In 1976 the choir school was in crisis, with only 36 pupils, aged between eight and 13, two dozen of whom were choristers in the Abbey choir and the other 12 probationers. The headmaster, 'a very agreeable, dedicated man' who nevertheless lacked 'any real grip on the running of the school,' was replaced the following year by an outstanding headmaster, Michael Keall, who remained in the post a decade and formed a very close relationship with Edward. 'No headmaster ever venerated his chairman of governors more than I did,' Keall wrote to the author on 11 June 2000. '[Edward] cared passionately about the school ... and gave me the inspiration of his constant affection for it and deep interest in its affairs.' Michael Keall was one of many connected with the Abbey who have never forgotten a kind of catchall blessing Edward might bestow on anyone at any time, which quoted out of context sounds rather odd but became very much his personal leitmotiv: 'The afterglow of a cherished remembrance.'

On 25 November 1976 Edward received the first of two honorary degrees, a doctorate of divinity from London University at a ceremony presided over by the chancellor, Queen Elizabeth the Queen Mother. It was to be another three years before Donald Coggan, archbishop of Canterbury since 1974, got around to conferring on Edward an honorary Lambeth doctorate in divinity, in recognition of his 'Service to Westminster Abbey since 1951 and as Dean, and in gratitude for his writings.'

The year 1976 also saw the publication of a book with the apposite title *Man of Christian Action*, the man in question being Canon John Collins of Christian Action. It was published by Lutterworth Press, edited by Ian Henderson, and consisted of contributions from a galaxy of distinguished writers (J B Priestley, Father Thomas Corbishley, a highly regarded Jesuit, Trevor Huddleston, Iris Murdoch) on the various aspects of Canon Collins's life and work, and among those who were asked to join in the celebration was Edward. He recalled that 'For relatively young men, fed up with violence and anxious to build bridges instead of knocking them down and concerned to make Christian faith (however they understood it) a reality in the social, economic and political life of their neighbourhood and nation, Christian Action seemed the answer. To such John Collins became a symbol embodying this hope and his movement the expression of their collective will.'

And he took the opportunity of expressing perhaps more forthrightly than he had done anywhere else his abhorrence of and moral objections to capital punishment, even though in the United Kingdom it had already been abolished.

> I have always regarded capital punishment as an impiety which outrages and does violence to specifically Christian insights. It seems to me inter alia to deny the Christian doctrine of redemption, to write off the significance of the time world and to usurp a divine prerogative in the absolute judgement in which it engages. To me this is transparently clear, so much so that I regard every judicial execution as saying publicly, 'The Christian faith is not true.' (This does not mean, of course, that there are not other and cogent reasons to deplore capital punishment.) However, in stumping the country on behalf of the campaign for its abolition I soon found that my view was by no means acceptable to a large number of Christians. Indeed it was often in these circles that the desire to retain it seemed strongest, so much so that to further the cause it was often wiser to avoid references to Christian faith. As to the cause of abolition, humanists in general proved far more sympathetic and suggestive.

After preaching against capital punishment at Putney one evening, and then conducting a discussion on the matter, Edward noted in his diary, 'No subject elicits more unreason. I marshalled the massive evidence which (I think) conclusively illustrates - so far as such evidence can illustrate it - that the death penalty is no deterrent. Yet one silly ass, with what was meant to be great sarcasm, observed that prisons would soon be like Butlin Holiday Camps.' In his article in *Man of Christian Action* Edward admitted to the failure of a Christian Action conference he had chaired on road safety. 'No cause deserves more support,' he wrote, 'for the criminality of some road users leads to countless deaths and untold suffering ... We spent an agreeable day, but if my memory serves me well almost the only publicity given to it was the observation of a Roman priest that he always said a short prayer to St Christopher when crossing a London street. A happy day but nothing really came of it!'

No greater contrast in Abbey ceremonial could be illustrated than by a memorial service held on 30 March 1977 for Janani Luwum, archbishop of Uganda, who had been murdered by the hideous dictator of that country, Idi Amin, only to be followed a week later by the distribution of Maundy money by the Queen. On 1 July the Queen played hostess to the dean and Chapter when, as 'a privileged body', they were summoned to Buckingham Palace wearing their scarlet cassocks, preaching bands, gowns, scarves and academic hoods to present a loyal address on the occasion of the Queen's Silver Jubilee. Thus adorned they piled into the Choir School's rusty minibus. Having arrived at 9.30am for a rehearsal, it was lunch time before their turn came round, the legal secretary reading the address inscribed on vellum. They were back at the Palace to present a Loyal Address in July 1981 on the occasion of the engagement of the Prince of Wales, when they expressed their sadly misplaced confidence that through the Grace of God the 'relationship of mutual trust and sacrificial self-giving' shared by Prince Charles and Lady Diana Spencer would 'encourage the younger generation to build a world more compassionate and caring.'

Edward's own contribution to quirkiness was in evidence in the summer of 1977 when he invited Sir Arthur Bryant to preach, at some length, what had become known, since its inception in 1965 as part of the Abbey's 900th anniversary, as the One People Oration; every year since, 900 people had been invited to hear some noteworthy person preach, and then to take a glass of wine in the garden. Supposing every guest did only drink one glass, a highly unlikely supposition, at £3 a bottle the cost in 1977 of this one function alone could not have been less than £450. But the really odd thing is that apparently Edward, a left-wing pacifist, regarded Bryant, the archetypal jingoistic right-winger and pre-war admirer of Hitler, as 'possibly the greatest living English historian and thought he would be a particularly appropriate orator during this Silver Jubilee Year.'[12] Another One Person Orator Edward thought appropriate in July 1979 was the ITV news reader Anna Ford, who turned up in a see-through dress.

Just before Christmas Edward received from one of the Lay Vicars an abusive letter, criticising his decision to abandon sung matins on Fridays. Edward had been prompted to reduce the workload of the choir because Michael Keall had expressed 'unease at the degree of pressure being imposed on the choristers by the increased number of special services.'[13] Canon Beeson had opposed this move. 'Now Friday has gone and Tuesday is sure to follow - sooner rather than later, I fear' he noted in his diary. Sure enough, sung matins was scrapped at the end of July 1981.

On 14 March 1973, while still archdeacon, Edward had conducted a service of blessing in St Faith's Chapel for the leader of the Liberal Party, Jeremy Thorpe, and his second wife, formerly the Countess of Harewood; Thorpe's first marriage, conducted in the chapel at Lambeth Palace by Michael Ramsey, had ended in tragedy when his wife was killed in a car crash, and Marion Harewood's marriage to the Queen's cousin had ended in Lord Harewood's adultery and divorce. Hence Thorpe and Lady Harewood had been married at a civil ceremony prior to the Abbey blessing.

Edward could never have dreamed that in 1978 he would be involved, if only indirectly, in the drama of Thorpe's arrest and trial for murder. Edward became involved through his friendship with Nadir Dinshaw, a wealthy Parsee, Harrow educated, an ardent Anglophile and a resident of Jersey, who had been introduced to the Carpenters by Joost de Blank; in time there were not many well known or influential members of the Establishment with whom Dinshaw was not at least on terms of acquaintanceship. One such was Thorpe, an overweeningly ambitious politician to whom, most unfortunately, Nadir entrusted a generous measure of his friendship. Another was David Steel, Thorpe's successor as leader of the Liberal Party, who, in his extremely readable autobiography, *Against Goliath*,[14] describes Dinshaw as 'my great friend.' Steel first met Dinshaw in 1968 when he and his wife were lunching at the House of Commons with Thorpe and his first wife, Caroline. After Caroline's death Dinshaw did much to support and console Thorpe. It therefore came to David Steel as 'an unpleasant shock' when at dinner on 9 March 1976 Nadir Dinshaw told him that two years earlier, at a time, as everyone now knows, Thorpe was in deep trouble over his relationship with a young unstable stable boy by the name of Norman Scott, Thorpe had asked Dinshaw if he would deposit £10,000 in his Jersey account and use the money to defray various election expenses. Thorpe's explanation for this somewhat unusual request was that a property developer in the Bahamas, Jack Hayward (who was later to give evidence for the prosecution when Thorpe was accused of conspiracy and incitement to murder), wanted anonymity - which later turned out to be one of Thorpe's many lies. He later pretended that Dinshaw was an accountant who had agreed to pay out any 'ambiguous expenses.'

Thorpe attempted to launder a second sum of £10,000 by using Dinshaw as an unwitting dupe, and it was after he had parted with £7,500 which he discovered had been used to purchase incriminating letters relating to Thorpe and his former friend Scott that Dinshaw went first to Edward Carpenter for advice and later that evening confided in Steel. Edward's advice was immediately to return the remaining £2,500.

In April 1978 Nadir Dinshaw had the unnerving experience of being questioned by the police, and the even more unpleasant experience of being lent on by Thorpe, who told him to pretend he had some business dealings with Hayward. When Dinshaw refused to lie, Thorpe 'suggested that he would be asked "to move on"' - as Steel remarked, 'a crude and foolish threat and poor return for the staunch friendship that Nadir had shown him.' It was small wonder that Dinshaw, who later was obliged to give evidence at the Old Bailey against Thorpe and was totally exonerated by the trial judge, felt in need of moral support from Christian friends like

Edward and Trevor Beeson, whom he also knew well. It was entirely in character with his generous spirit that for many summers Dinshaw placed his Jersey home at the disposal of the Carpenter family so that they could have summer holidays by the sea.

Visitors to the Abbey were nothing if not varied. On 2 April 1978, at the invitation of Trevor Beeson, a female canon from the USA clambered into the pulpit; 10 May saw a call being made by Shenouda III, a Coptic patriarch who called himself Pope of Alexandria; on 13 June Beeson found himself shaking hands 'with an unusually wicked man, namely Nicholas Ceaucesceu, the President of Romania.' He was on a state visit at the instigation of the Government, which almost automatically included a wreath laying ceremony at the grave of the Unknown Warrior. His visit must have brought home to Edward just how impossible it was to get out of certain unpleasant duties if you were running a Royal Peculiar. 'Ceaucesceu looks a nasty, ruthless piece of work,' Beeson noted.[15] It must have been even more unpleasant for the Queen and the Duke of Edinburgh to have this creature to stay, and, at the request of the Foreign Secretary, for the Queen to invest him as an Honorary Knight Grand Cross of the Civil Division of the Order of the Bath. Three days before he was summarily executed by his own people in December 1989, on Foreign and Commonwealth Office advice the award was cancelled, and the insignia was returned to the Central Chancery of the Orders of Knighthood by the Romanian Government in 1994.

One of the toughest pastoral - as well as administrative - headaches with which Edward had to deal as dean was the addiction to the bottle of Nicholas MacMichael, Keeper of the Muniments. His being an expert on the archives could not be allowed to excuse erratic behaviour in the Bookshop or falling down flat on the pavement, and at Christmas 1978 Edward felt obliged to suspend him from duty. MacMichael, who died in November 1985 at the age of 52, was not the only inebriate discovered in the Abbey in Edward's day. In June 1980, during a choir practice, the director of another London choir tried, not too coherently, to interfere with the conductor, Douglas Guest, and was deposited in Victoria Street by one of the vergers. There he was arrested and charged with being drunk and disorderly. When he appeared at Bow Street Magistrates' Court who should turn up to speak on his behalf but Edward, who did so 'so eloquently and so convincingly' that the stipendary magistrate found the accused Not Guilty.[16]

Holidays in 1979, in Japan and at Nadir Dinshaw's house in Jersey, must have come as a welcome break. Edward was by now fairly well travelled. In May 1965 he and Lilian had journeyed via Egypt and Ceylon to Australia, staying in archiepiscopal lodgings at both Perth and

Melbourne. They were by the lake of Galilee in 1972 and again in 1977. In 1976 they were in Italy; in 1978, after visits to Frankfurt and Bombay, they arrived in Thailand. The following year they flew Pan Am to Peking, calling at Hong Kong and Tokyo, making trips to the Great Wall of China and the Imperial Palace. A tour of San Francisco, Los Angeles and Las Vegas was undertaken in October 1982, Lake Como and Assisi were visited in 1988, and only two years before his death Edward was back in Italy.

On 20 May 1979 Lilian found herself thrust into one of the most ghastly pastoral situations it is possible to imagine. A mere 10 months previously, on 29 July 1978, Trevor and Josephine Beeson's younger daughter Catherine had been married at the High Altar to Anthony Andrews, son of the Abbey's clerk of works. Now Lilian had been deputed to greet the Beesons at the ticket barrier at Liverpool Street Station on their return from a weekend in Durham to break the news that their 25-year-old son-in-law had been killed that lunchtime in a motor accident. She did so, according to Trevor Beeson, 'in her characteristically gentle way.' Edward, who had married the couple, conducted Anthony's funeral 'with great sensitivity.' In considerably happier circumstances, 4 July 1983 saw Catherine Andrews back at the High Altar when she married the chaplain to the Abbey, Charles Taylor. Trevor Beeson gave away his daughter for a second time, and Edward celebrated the Eucharist. This must surely have been the first time in history that anyone had been married twice at the High Altar of Westminster Abbey.

Another family tragedy, one on a truly epic scale, brought a sense of grandeur yet desolation to the Abbey in September 1979 with the state funeral of Earl Mountbatten, assassinated by the IRA while on holiday, along with his daughter's mother-in-law, one of his grandsons and a young friend of the family. Being semi-royal (Mountbatten's father had been a Battenberg prince, his mother a granddaughter of Queen Victoria) the earl had left meticulous instructions about his funeral, carried out by Edward to the letter, Edward having been recalled from a holiday in Jersey; Reg Pullen, the Receiver General, likewise had to be summoned home from France. On 3 September Trevor Beeson noted in his diary, 'Westminster Abbey and its precincts have been turned into a fortress.' The funeral was to be attended by most of the royal family, foreign royalty, exiled royalty, overseas heads of state, leading politicians, and the IRA were in a murderous mood. Not even the canons could enter the Abbey without identity cards. Cars were banned from Dean's Yard and the whole atmosphere became 'crisis-ridden.' At the funeral the Prince of Wales, whose mentor Mountbatten had been, could scarcely manage to read Psalm 107.

On 7 September, two days after Mountbatten's funeral, it was announced that Robert Runcie, bishop of St Albans, was to be the new archbishop of Canterbury, and he paid his first visit to the Abbey as archbishop on 1 May for a consecration. Traditionally a Protest is read when a new archbishop (and sometimes a new bishop of London) makes his first visit, an ancient reminder that neither have any jurisdiction in or over the Abbey - which of course they already perfectly well know. Runcie had first encountered Edward in the late 1950s when he heard him speak at St Edward's Church in Cambridge, and although in anticipation of the new archbishop's first visit to the Abbey the Chapter had decided to modify the wording of the Protest somewhat, so that it did not sound too unfriendly, Trevor Beeson noted in his diary that when the Protest was read 'the Archbishop seemed distinctly unamused.'[16] Yet in a letter to the author written very shortly before he died, Lord Runcie said, 'Edward was one of the most Christian gentlemen I have ever known and he was kindness itself to me when I became Archbishop and had to appear at Westminster Abbey. I well remember how apologetic he was about "The Complaint" which has to be read out by the Dean on the first appearance of a new Archbishop - reminding him that he has no authority in the Abbey.

'He immediately made his spare bedroom available to me as a dressing room and a place of peace and quiet before emerging into the Jerusalem Chamber to meet others who were preparing for some big service. He was always anxious for my comfort and clearly eager that the service should be worthy of the occasion rather than that it should promote his own position as a consummate composer of Bidding Prayers.'[17] A minor hiatus occurred however in March 1982 when Archbishop Runcie was due to preach at the unveiling of a memorial stone to all who had died in the twentieth century in the causes of justice, freedom and peace. He had brought his chaplain and primatal cross on a previous occasion, but this time the Chapter decided he could not appear to exercise some sort of archiepiscopal jurisdiction, so Edward was requested to ask Runcie to come alone.

No better example of Edward's gifts as a 'consummate composer of Bidding Prayers,' referred to by Lord Runcie, could have been found than in the sensitive and comprehensive Bidding Prayer he wrote for Eric Abbott's memorial service, held on 8 July 1983. 'We meet here in Westminster Abbey where the remains of all that could be mortal of Eric Abbott have been interred, to give thanks to God, to whom be the glory, for a rare person who across the years ministered to many; supported them in faith and un-faith; identified himself with them in their joys and sorrows and in so doing mediated the love of Christ who was to him the way, the truth and the life. We recall Eric's graces of personality, his subtle and sometimes impish humour, his unfailing sense of style. We remember with gratitude that in counselling he was shrewd and unshockable, recreating hope and generating expectancy. We pay tribute to his distinguished and selfless service in many institutions which he administered with understanding and efficiency, thanking God for the vision which made him see their corporate life as fulfilled in the loving, personal demands of Christ and his kingdom.

'We pray for those, his special friends, amongst whom we think of John, who as they drew sustenance from Eric gave back to him a deep and abiding affection. May he who often defied the crippling power of illness, while using it for a well from which others could draw water, enter into the joy of that kingdom for which, during his earthly pilgrimage, he laboured and longed...'

After interviewing five outstanding candidates for the vacant post of organist and master of the choristers, in June 1980 Edward and his colleagues took a calculated gamble on appointing the organist and Lecturer in Music at Christ Church, Simon Preston, a post he had held since 1970; it was a gamble because they had been warned 'about a degree of prima donna-ism in him.' He was installed on 15 May the following year, and immediately won plaudits from the Chapter for his conducting of the choir. But before long Preston was complaining about insufficient rehearsal time and poor discipline, among the men as well as the boys. There developed almost inevitable clashes between Preston and the Choir School headmaster, Preston's concern being to have choirboys rehearsing for as many hours as possible, the headmaster's to make sure enough time was preserved for educational purposes; the bone of contention between Simon Preston and the Chapter was to become the amount of time he might reasonably give to outside activities.

Simon Preston's pessimistic annual reports to the Chapter would have seriously disturbed a body who were not entirely confident of his musical genius and were prepared to take the rough with the smooth. 'I would like to say how difficult it is to work in Westminster Abbey' his January 1984 report began. He claimed he had no ready access to the Chapter 'over difficult matters', and went on to complain about the 'mounting number of hymns which are being sung to the detriment of the choral tradition.' There was no acknowledgement of the sum the Chapter had just spent on music - £235,000 in 1983, not taking into account a further £400,000 they were planning to spend rebuilding the organ. But Preston's complaints never marred personal relationships.

'Something of a crisis has blown up over the question of the Organist's absences from the Abbey' Trevor Beeson wrote on 28 February 1985. It was, he added, 'a matter which has been causing concern for some time.' The ins and outs of the controversy are complicated and happily enveloped in the mists of time, but in a nutshell they concerned the amount of leave Simon Preston was permitted, and the extent to which he required consent from the dean to undertake overseas engagements. The saga is related in some detail in Beeson's diaries, and although Beeson gives due credit to Preston's great talents, and is aware that his artistic interests would naturally come before his concern for administration, he is quite clear that Edward was 'being taken for a ride and his charitable view of human nature was being exploited.' It is only right therefore to record that in a letter to the author the Precentor at the time, Canon Alan Luff, has written:

> ...before coming [Simon Preston] negotiated with the Chapter that he should have the summer term off in alternate years. This was not put into [his] contract but there was an exchange of letters of intent, which I saw. The time away was to be 'paid for' by his putting in extra work in the other five terms. This was not difficult to do against the standard set by his predecessor, who was not to be seen on routine Abbey business from after Sunday services until Thursday Evensong. Simon in fact would often do all the services in the week, to the chagrin of the second and third organists who would expect their share of the limelight.
>
> When however he came to the beginning of the year in which he expected to be away, and was making arrangements for a tour, some members of the Chapter took fright and began saying that he could not do this. The kind of argument that was deployed was, 'What if the Queen Mother dies!' Bishop Knapp-Fisher was particularly vehement, and in general anti-Preston.
>
> I remonstrated with Edward Carpenter on Simon's behalf, since I had seen the letter setting up the arrangement. EC's only argument was, 'Yes, I know we said that, but it really is unthinkable.' It is the only time that I ever found him less than most scrupulously honourable in his undertakings'[18]

It also has to be said, in fairness to Simon Preston, a musician of international stature whom the Abbey were fortunate to have on their staff until 1987, that he had previously served, from 1962 (when he was 24) until 1967, as sub-organist under Douglas Guest, and Edward knew perfectly well the potential drawbacks when appointing him master of the choristers in 1980. Indeed, in his diary for 9 November 1966 he had written, 'Meeting of Chapter and Deanery with Douglas apropos Simon Preston. Guest stated his case admirably and was much more restrained than I thought he would be. SP, he said, was brilliant, but nerve-wracking to work with. He never answered letters and no one ever knew where he was.

With so many rows of one sort or another breaking out among cathedral staff in recent years - the scandal of Lincoln's long-running battles was probably the most damaging, unless you happen to believe the mishandled sacking in 1998 of Martin Neary from Westminster Abbey deserves the label - one should not be too surprised to learn that Edward Carpenter's time as dean of Westminster witnessed some petty squabbles. For no matter how kindly or sensitive a dean or provost may be, the cloistered world of cathedrals can all too easily become claustrophobic whirlpools of ecclesiastical amour propre. 'A most almighty row is raging between the Senior Lay Vicar and the Clerk of the Works' Trevor Beeson recorded in his diary on 23 July 1980. Solicitors' letters flew around on this unhappy occasion. By the autumn, the Senior Lay Vicar was complaining about the alleged left-wing content of Abbey sermons, and he was proposing to send a letter to the *Daily Telegraph* 'couched in the most rude terms, and containing several inaccuracies.' Canon Sebastian Charles, clearly not in the best of health, was causing anxiety by his frequent absences. With his tact, sensitivity and the general atmosphere of tolerance and friendliness he created, Edward was usually able to contain these problems before they escalated.

A visit from Queen Elizabeth the Queen Mother on 26 November 1980 to celebrate her 80th birthday must have promised a tranquil respite. After listening to an anthem, Queen Elizabeth repaired to the Jerusalem Chamber, where she was handed a statutory glass of gin and tonic. The story of how Edward, after proposing her health, snatched up the royal glass and downed it has passed into legend.

The reason behind this faux pas (as with the muddle he could get into at the altar) was not so much eccentricity as short-sightedness, and Trevor Beeson has recorded that the Queen Mother led the uproarious laughter. 'And the beauty of it was that Edward seemed in no way embarrassed.' It was, Beeson added, 'a classic example of the way in which Edward treats everyone alike and is quite unfazed by the status of those whose company he keeps.'

13 January 1981: 'The Dean - that kindest and most enthusiastic of men - wants us to join the chorus of praise for Fred Housego, the winner of the recent BBC Mastermind contest. Housego and his wife were invited to have drinks and bits with the Dean and Chapter and their wives at lunchtime today and Edward presented him with an inscribed copy of Dean Stanley's *Memorials of Westminster Abbey*.' Mr Housego, billed as a London taxi driver, had caused a sensation by answering questions on

the Abbey, but it transpired that as well as being a cabbie he was also a London Tourist Board Blue Badge Guide who specialised in knowledge of the Abbey. Edward was so swept up with the general approbation that he wanted Housego to open an exhibition in the library to mark the centenary of the birth of Dean Stanley, and even to present the prizes at the Choir School Speech Day.

Since the duke and duchess of York broke with family tradition by getting married in the Abbey, five other members of the royal family had chosen the Abbey for a public celebration of their nuptials: George duke of Kent in 1934, Princess Elizabeth in 1947, Princess Margaret in 1960, Princess Alexandra in 1963 and Princess Anne in 1973. (In 1935 the duke of Gloucester had been married in the private chapel at Buckingham Palace, very possibly because his bride, Lady Alice Montagu-Douglas-Scott, was too shy to face the ordeal of a public ceremony, and in 1961 Edward duke of Kent had been married in York Minster, for the good reason that his bride came from a landed Yorkshire family, and her father was a local Lord Lieutenant.) So a visit from the private secretary to the Prince of Wales in February 1981, to inform Edward that His Royal Highness intended marrying Lady Diana Spencer in St Paul's Cathedral, came as a very considerable shock. Trevor Beeson says the luckless courtier, Edward Adeane, broke the news in 'a none too courteous manner.'[19] He may of course have been dreading his mission, and wishing his royal master had had the courtesy to write to Edward or even visit him himself. The explanations Adeane offered were that the prince had been very impressed by the Service of Thanksgiving for the Queen Mother held at St Paul's the previous year and that he believed the unrestricted sightline up the nave of St Paul's would afford a better view for the congregation than could have been obtained in the Abbey, the High Altar and Choir being cut off from the nave by the Choir Screen.

These were arguments that cut little ice with Edward, who thought the prince's decision, even though it was one he was perfectly entitled to make, was a slight on the Abbey. He felt keenly for the Abbey staff, especially Reg Pullen, who would have relished the whole thing and organised it well, and the choir, whose extra earnings would have been considerable. But considerable too would have been the cost to the Abbey of financing the most spectacular royal wedding ever held; closure of the Abbey for several days in preparation for Lord Mountbatten's funeral had resulted in a loss of income estimated at £9,000, a sum the Treasury seemed in no mood to reimburse. At the time of the Queen Mother's Thanksgiving Service in 2000 for her 100th birthday it was alleged that St Paul's Cathedral was trying to recoup from the Treasury £15,000, and readers of *The Times* were reminded that the wedding of the Prince of

Wales had cost a staggering £500,000, so at the end of the day Westminster Abbey may have had a lucky let out.

Nevertheless Edward was anxious for the Chapter jointly to send a letter to the Queen expressing their concern at the decision to abandon the Abbey, and Reg Pullen was led to believe by the Lord Chamberlain that such a letter would not be unwelcome. But the Chapter was unable to agree on tactics, Bishop Knapp-Fisher expressing the view that no letter should go at all, and in the end Edward decided to write off his own bat. It was some three or four weeks before he received a fairly non-committal reply from the Queen's assistant private secretary, Robert Fellowes, brother-in-law of Lady Diana, a delay which might indicate the difficulty the Palace had experienced, trying to support the concerns of the Abbey without appearing to be at loggerheads with the prince. In the meantime, the Queen turned up for the Maundy Thursday service, on 16 April, and she took that opportunity of expressing her appreciation of the service 'in the warmest of terms', mentioning especially the choir's 'outstanding contribution' and going out of her way to instruct her private secretary to say that she was 'never less than highly impressed by the beauty and precision with which the ceremony turns out at Westminster Abbey.'[20] Edward took this to be a coded 'reassurance to the Abbey', which undoubtedly it was. What seems the most likely explanation for the choice of St Paul's is that Prince Charles may well have felt qualms about his marriage being celebrated in the Abbey while his experience of his great-uncle's funeral there remained so raw. Had he expressed these sentiments in person to Edward he would of course have received a sympathetic response.

At the end of June the XIVth Dalai Lama, spiritual leader of Tibet, arrived at the Deanery for a five day visit. Edward could scarcely have been pushing inter-faith frontiers at the Abbey out any further. His Holiness arrived in a cohort of Land Rovers accompanied by security guards and monks who immediately took up positions in the hall and outside the Dalai Lama's bedroom. Imagining their esteemed visitor shared their own preference for vegetarian food, Edward and Lilian were somewhat taken aback when His Holiness requested bacon and eggs for breakfast. On the day before his departure the Abbey clergy were invited to a formal meeting in the drawing room. Trevor Beeson has left an all too believable account of this somewhat frigid exercise.

'He was seated in a large chair near the centre of the room and we took it in turns to occupy a chair alongside him. Conversation was by no means easy. I put to him the by no means original question, "What do you believe to be the most important issue facing the world today?" After a long pause came the reply, "Peace." "How does Your Holiness

believe this can be achieved?" Another long pause. "By seeking unity."
"How is unity to be achieved?" A longer pause. "Through compassion
and tolerance."' The previous evening the Dalai Lama had addressed an
audience of 2,000 in Central Hall and it seems they were 'entranced by
his presence and message.'[21]

In the summer of 1984 the Dalai Lama made his third visit to England
and once again stayed at the Deanery. Jerusalem Chamber was booked
for two evenings so that he could give parties. He planned to teach in
Camden, travel to Scotland via Ampleforth College in north Yorkshire
and to speak informally in the Abbey. This he did in fragmented English
and the dialogue was much on a par with the one experienced by Trevor
Beeson in 1981. He was anxious to meet the Prince of Wales, the Speaker
of the House of Commons, Metropolitan Anthony of the Orthodox
Church, resident in London, and boys from Westminster School. Edward's
welcome to the Dalai Lama combined his interest in inter-faith dialogue
and his concern to highlight the current plight of the Tibetan people.

The year 1984 opened with one of the most remarkable services
ever held in the Abbey, to mark the 40th anniversary of the ordination
to the priesthood of the first woman priest in the Anglican Communion,
Florence Tim Oi Li. She had been ordained entirely on his own initiative
during the war - and owing to emergency circumstances - by the bishop of
Hong Kong. It was not until 1970 that her ordination was regularised, the
Communists having meanwhile forced her to work as a manual labourer.
Although as far back as 1976 Edward had introduced female honorary
stewards into the Abbey, the Movement for the Ordination of Women
still had much campaigning to do before women would be ordained in
the Church of England. It was the Movement who organised the service,
and so many people turned up that Edward led the scramble to produce
more chairs, an occasion that prompted the dean emeritus of St Paul's,
Alan Webster, to describe him as a 'leader who was always there.'[22]
Edward read a message from Robert Runcie, a lukewarm supporter of
the ordination of women, which nevertheless included the remark, 'Your
selfless ministry is an example to us all.'

For many years Edward had bicycled to Gilmore House on Clapham
Common to lecture, free of charge, to the women students on English
Church History. His lectures have been recalled by a former Principal,
Deaconess Janet Grierson, as 'brilliant - given without any notes, and the
students were enthralled. He was strongly in favour of women priests and
was appalled even then at the limitations imposed on Deaconesses.'

Edward was now 73 but under no obligation to retire; he had only
been dean a decade. There were some, including Trevor Beeson, who felt
he was beginning to show a marked deterioration in his grip on Abbey

affairs, in no area more obviously than in his dangerous reluctance to sort out incompetent colleagues. Almost since the date of his appointment as a canon, in 1978 as successor to David Edwards, Sebastian Charles had failed to fit in, partly because of his obvious health problem. Except when on duty in the Abbey Canon Charles never seemed to be around, unaccustomed as he was to the demands of communal daily worship. Grave doubts had been felt by everyone about his ability to take on the role of Treasurer when Trevor Beeson resigned on being appointed Rector of St Margaret's and Speaker's Chaplain. But no one else was available, and in the event he did rather well. But on 9 March 1984 Trevor Beeson recorded in his diary, 'Sebastian Charles, our Treasurer, was once again absent from the Chapter because of unspecified indisposition. These absences, combined with failure to keep engagements and an apparent inability on some occasions to grasp the essentials of a discussion, are becoming a great worry. In his own interests, as well as those of the Abbey, this problem - which seems to have a health dimension - needs to be tackled. But the Dean, who is the only member of the Chapter who can do this, evidently feels unable to grasp the nettle.' Perhaps Edward felt that blame was evenly spread. In 1981 he recorded in his diary that in the past two years 39 meetings of the Chapter had been held, from 20 of which at least one member was absent.

In April 1984 Beeson thought Edward's powers were 'fading quite rapidly', although this may have had something to do with failing eyesight. Indeed it was in this period as dean that Edward showed tact and wisdom in his handling of the departure of John Rae as headmaster of Westminster School. To complicate matters, the sub-dean, Edward Knapp-Fisher, having reached the age of 69, wanted to plan his own retirement for when he was 70 but felt unable to do so as he had no idea when an interregnum might occur, requiring his presence to see in a new dean. As so often happens when great men are reaching the end of the road - Garbett of York and Winston Churchill are obvious examples - no one could bring themselves to say it was time to go. In his diary, Trevor Beeson confessed: 'I am close to Edward and might well be the best person to speak to him, but for some reason - I suppose it is cowardice - I don't feel able to do so. This is partly for fear of hurting someone who has himself always avoided painful confrontation with others.'

While he was dean, Edward took every occasion possible to enhance the physical aspects of the Abbey. Within months of her death in 1976, Edward had a memorial to Dame Sybil Thorndike, with an epitaph written by J B Priestly, unveiled. In October the following year he took the opportunity of the unveiling, by Lady Fisher, of a new memorial near the site of the Tudor half-sisters, the Catholic Mary I and the Protestant Elizabeth I, to preach a sermon in which he expressed impatience at the slowness of the ecumenical movement. At least he was spared the Vatican's crass pronouncement in the year 2000 that the Church of England was not a 'proper' Church. During the course of a concert devoted to his music, on 21 November 1978 Edward organised the unveiling of a memorial stone to Benjamin Britten, close to those recalling two of England's greatest composers, Elgar and Vaughan Williams.

It must have been with a sore heart that in 1980 Edward felt obliged to decline an offer from the Byron Society of a bust of the poet, for in 1969 the Poetry Society had already contributed towards a marble memorial in the floor of Poets' Corner - and no one is permitted two memorials in the Abbey. On 24 February 1981 Edward adventurously permitted a rock band to perform, an occasion - apart from the litter left by the television crews - generally agreed to have gone off remarkably well. Amid some controversy, on 1 March (St David's Day) 1982 a memorial to the often drunken Dylan Thomas was unveiled. When the George Bernard Shaw Society objected to a memorial to an avowed atheist (Shaw had himself left instructions that he did not want a memorial in Westminster Abbey) Edward backed off. Noel Coward was quite another matter, partly because Edward was keen to utilise the South Choir Aisle, where Sybil Thorndike's memorial had been placed, to commemorate actors and actresses, and in April 1984 the Queen Mother, a friend as well as a fan of Coward's, was easily persuaded to perform the unveiling.

A Victorian dean whom Edward greatly admired was William Buckland, and in 1985 he decided to have restored his portrait and the desk he used when dean, between the years 1845 and 1856. Buckland's eccentricity put Edward's in the shade. Buckland was both cleric and scientist. Being a great believer in practical experience, he was said to have eaten his way through the entire animal kingdom, proclaiming the mole the nastiest thing he had ever tasted until he tried a blue-bottle.

Like Edward and Lilian, Dean Buckland and his wife kept open house at the Deanery, where, using his scientific knowledge, he had pipe drains installed, the first of their kind in London. He also took an interest in the catering at the school, and appointed a new cook, who introduced the boys to puddings; they failed to find favour with the boys however, and Buckland 'had them thrown at his head.'[23]

Edward's finest hour as memorialist came after he had announced his pending retirement. On Armistice Day 1985 a memorial to 16 First World War poets, including, inevitably, Wilfred Owen, Siegfried Sassoon, Robert Graves, Edmund Blunden and Rupert Brooke, was unveiled, in the presence of Ted Hughes, the Poet Laureate. Edward's obituary in *The Times* made the point that much of his faith he owed to English literature.

'He strove to persuade the Church that poets were needed not only in the calendar and in the readings at liturgies but in the search for faith. He believed that there could be no Decade of Evangelism without an opening of minds and hearts to poetry and drama.' Edward particularly revered the war poets because they were, he said, the first people to speak the truth about the Great War.

There had been numerous occasions when Edward experienced an anguished conflict between his pacifism and what he believed to be his obligation to open the Abbey to everyone. Services held for NATO and the Royal Air Force had held the threat, smoothed over in the event, of swords, rifles and fixed bayonets being paraded. As a pacifist, Edward, as dean, found himself having to compromise his principles in a fairly dramatic manner at installations of new Knights of the Bath, laying their swords on the altar and then returning them with the words: 'I exhort and admonish you to use your sword to the Glory of God, in defence of the Gospel, the maintenance of your Sovereign's right and honour, and for all equity and justice to the utmost of your power.' When Marshal of the Royal Air Force Sir Arthur Harris, better known as 'Bomber' Harris, died in 1984, Edward flatly refused to read the Bidding Prayer at the Abbey memorial service to which, as a Knight Grand Cross of the Order of the Bath, he was entitled. It was Harris, carrying out government policy, who oversaw the obliteration of Dresden, his actions proving so controversial he was denied a peerage. But Edward's major conflict with the Establishment came the following year, when without consultation with anyone the headstrong prime minister, Margaret Thatcher, blithely announced in the House of Commons there would be a service in the Abbey to commemorate the 40th anniversary of Victory in Europe Day. Such discourtesy was bad enough, but when Mrs Thatcher went on to demand that no foreigners other than ambassadors were to be invited Edward's patience snapped and Peter Hitchens, the political correspondent of the *Daily Express*, wrote an article on 3 May stating 'A major row is brewing over next week's service at Westminster Abbey to commemorate V E day.'

Meanwhile, Edward had formed an inter-Church committee, and on 8 May Church leaders from Japan, East and West Germany, Poland, Russia, Holland, France and the USA carried candles while children from the Royal Ballet School danced from the Great West Door to the Sacrarium. Thanksgiving, penitence, reconciliation and healing were the themes of a liturgical amalgam from which the Precentor, Alan Luff, created a coherent act of worship attended by the Queen and watched by millions throughout the world on television, and Edward's disdain of triumphalism set the tone for Archbishop Runcie's refusal - much to Mrs Thatcher's disgust - to boast of victory at St Paul's after the Falklands War. Writing to the dean, Dr Wesley Carr, on 12 June 2000, Canon Luff, one of the most creative Precentors who has ever worked at the Abbey, said, 'Half of my time at the Abbey was under Edward. It was an amazing experience. It was a time of great development liturgically at the Abbey. Edward, though shrewd in comment on all things, did not count himself a liturgist, so that I had a great responsibility in seeing the ASB brought into use. What survives from that period may now not seem very exciting, but we were in fact moving a great way. When I arrived, special services had not moved much beyond being Matins with a special prayer and sermon. With Edward's encouragement I was able more and more to devise orders of service for most occasions, and the prayers regularly became specially written litanies. The Sunday Evening Service became a time when a good deal of experiment was possible in music, drama and dance. I believe that everyone on the staff felt that same encouragement to use their gifts.'

By November 1985 Edward would be 75. He dreaded the thought of retirement because it would have been quite unseemly for him to be continuously popping back to keep in touch with what he regarded as his own extended family, the 100 or so employees of the Abbey; the ability to talk at any level to anyone was one of his rare gifts. 'I'd have loved to have gone on' he admitted, but already he was five years over the newly brought in statutory age of retirement, and after working on his Life of Fisher for 14 years in moments snatched from his duties as dean he realised it was time to go. On 9 July he told the Chapter he would be submitting his resignation to the prime minister with effect from 30 November. 'It was a moving moment,' Trevor Beeson recorded, '...and we were ... aware that the decision to retire was a painful one, because the Abbey is his life and he is bound to be bereft without it.

'Undoubtedly he has been a great dean.'

Eight

DADDY IS RELAXING

With Edward Carpenter's retirement made public there was inevitably speculation about his successor. A good many members of parliament thought Trevor Beeson should be appointed, but it was most unlikely the dean would be plucked from the Chapter twice running, and as Beeson was the first to admit, no present member of the Chapter could command unanimous support. In 1987 Beeson became dean of Winchester. The dean of Peterhouse, Cambridge, Edward Norman, was mentioned - in the cloisters at Westminster with baited breath, for his right-wing views appealed to Margaret Thatcher. Another conservative figure thought to be in with a chance was the headmaster of King's School, Canterbury, Peter Pilkington. It would have been unusual, but not unique, for a dean to be moved sideways, but Patrick Mitchell, the dean of Wells, was spoken of. In the event he became dean of Windsor. The one person no one seems to have considered, other than the prime minister's appointments secretary, now Robin Catford, was Michael Mayne, the vicar of the University Church of Great St Mary, Cambridge, who between 1959 and 1965 had served as the first of seven domestic chaplains to the bishop of Southwark, Mervyn Stockwood. Few people would have known that Mayne had previously turned down a bishopric; in 1975 Stockwood tried to woo him back to his diocese as suffragan bishop of Woolwich. The oddest feature of Michael Mayne's appointment to the deanery of Westminster, not only a prestigious but a very demanding post (it was announced from Downing Street on 7 January 1986), was that he was only just recovering from that mysterious and debilitating illness known as ME. He did recover, and became a successful and worthy successor to a fellow liberal. (Mayne's own successor, Wesley Carr, had the great misfortune shortly after his appointment to develop Parkinson's Disease.)

On 27 November 1985 Edward celebrated his 75th birthday, and the following day he and Lilian attended a farewell party in Up School, as the senior part of Westminster is known. Trevor Beeson was under no illusion that they were witnessing 'the passing of an era,' and that although by training and inclination Edward was an historian he would be remembered more as a 'modern churchman'. Under his leadership, Beeson wrote in his diary, 'The Abbey has become a much more warm and friendly place. The last vestiges of stuffiness and privilege have been removed, and many of those who come to share in our life express surprise and pleasure at the warmth of the welcome they receive.'

Before the party, Edward preached his last sermon as dean, and never even mentioned his departure. And when he was presented with a desk and a cheque he seemed covered with confusion and quite unable to grasp what all the fuss was about. This was entirely typical of Edward, for few men in public life have been so totally unselfish as he, so totally unaware of their own importance. This very marked side of Edward's character has given rise to a story that he declined to become dean emeritus. He did not decline a dean emeritus-ship for the simple reason he was never offered such an appointment. None of Edward's retired predecessors held the title dean emeritus, and there was never any question of Edward doing so. He quite rightly reverted to the style the Reverend Edward Carpenter.

What Edward did receive, in the personal gift of the sovereign, was Knight Commander of the Royal Victorian Order, the insignia merely being handed to him in a box by the Queen. He did not, for reasons previously explained, kneel to receive the accolade; hence Lilian, who was not invited to the private audience, did not become Lady Carpenter but remained Mrs Carpenter. It was at this quiet little ceremony that Edward returned to the Queen the badge he had worn as dean of the Order of the Bath. Freed from the constraints of marriage to a senior dignitary of the Church, Lilian felt able to pursue in greater depth her own quest for spiritual enlightenment, and some time after Edward's retirement she embraced the Bahá'i faith, founded in Iran as an offshoot of Shi'a Islam; Lilian believed the Bahá'i faith embraced all religious faiths, and Edward, with his usual tolerance, had explored the teachings of Lilian's new faith himself and believed that the Bahá'i faith and Christianity were not incompatible. Which, taking into account his commitment to the Inter-Faith Movement, was not very surprising. A United Nations report had stated that the Bahá'i faith was the world's fastest growing religion and Lilian was thought to be one of 6,000 adherents in Britain.

At the time of his retirement, Edward told a former chorister, James Wilkinson, that he had been commissioned to write three more books in addition to the Life of Fisher, still far from completion. One of these was his popular history of the Abbey, *Westminster Abbey*, referred to in Chapter Four, illuminated by brilliantly evocative pen and wash drawings by David Gentleman. The other two, real or imaginary, never materialised. Shortly after leaving the deanery Edward underwent two cataract operations and most of his active retirement was taken up completing the Fisher biography and seeing it to press. When Edward's father died in

1969 he bequeathed his house at Addlestone to Edward, which Edward now sold for £120,000, moving, on the proceeds, to a small terraced villa in Richmond, Surrey. A room on the first floor, overlooking the garden, was converted into an untidy study, booklined, needless to say, and here Edward tinkered away at Fisher for another five years. He had by now six grandchildren to give him pleasure (to whom he dedicated Fisher), and his concern for his one unmarried child, Paul, never slackened. On 28 September 1990 (the letter was both dated and legible!) he was writing to Paul to say, 'It seems a long time since I took you to the Athenaeum for a meal. I should like to repeat this! Would you? Let me know!'

Official invitations continued to arrive. 'In the gracious presence of Her Majesty the Queen, the Royal Patron of the Council of Christians and Jews' the Reverend Dr Edward Carpenter, KCVO was invited to a Reception at St James's Palace. In 1986 Edward had taken over from Lord Coggan as chairman of the Council of Christians and Jews, and with more time to spare in retirement he frequently travelled from Richmond to the West Hampstead offices of the Council. 'He could be slightly chaotic and disorganised,' the Director, Canon Jim Richardson, recalls, 'But somehow everything came together in a letter, or a talk at a meeting, that made perfect sense and was an excellent outline of the situation under discussion.'[1] Edward sometimes attended the parish church in Richmond, and new friends and neighbours were acquired. Edward told Nadir Dinshaw in an undated letter signed for him by Louise (and typed by her), 'we met Bishop Holloway at our local church here in Richmond the other week. He's quite a character, isn't he?' Which was quite an understatement. Richard Holloway was a sensationally controversial bishop of Edinburgh and Primus of the Episcopal Church in Scotland.

The absent-minded professor remained very much in evidence. In September 1990 Edward and Lilian went on holiday to the Dolomites. On a postcard from Deutschnofen Lilian told Paul, 'We had a bad journey, but have made up for it since. Daddy left his passport behind.' A friend had to be recruited to go back for it and they missed their train, 'so of course we missed the ferry and so the train [in France] ...We had to change twice. Once at Cologne, and the second time at Munich ... Daddy is relaxing.'

The year 1990 also found Edward in Rome, leading a delegation from the Council of Christians and Jews to meet the Pope. John Paul II told Edward he was deeply concerned about the danger of anti-semitism gaining ground again in Europe, and invited the Council to contribute ideas towards the formulation of Vatican policy. During this trip Edward was mugged in broad daylight outside the Coliseum. While a group of street children rummaged through his pockets he put up not the slightest resistance, looking in fact quite non-plussed, apparently not believing what was happening to him. The upshot was a stolen wallet – which had been empty.

The following year eventually saw the publication of Edward's Life of Fisher. Lady Fisher, as well as the subject of his labours (the book stretched to 820 pages, 773 of them text, and was published by a little known firm in Norwich, riddled with mistakes and at the preposterous price of £35), had now been dead 19 years, and three other archbishops of Canterbury, Ramsey, Coggan and Runcie, had been and gone. It was by 'kind permission of His Grace the Archbishop of Canterbury and Mrs Carey' that a Reception was held at Lambeth Palace on 5 December 1991 to mark the publication of Dr Edward Carpenter's 'long-awaited biography.' Wine was served - for just 60 minutes.

It seems odd that no obvious London publisher with a strong religious and biographical list like Cassell or Hodder and Stoughton would publish a book that with all its faults was always destined to make a major contribution to twentieth century ecclesiastical history; and had a firm experienced in handling a work inevitably containing a mountain of names, events and references, that demanded the most careful copy-editing and checking, published it, it might not have turned out looking like a dog's dinner. De La Warr is consistently misspelt. John Robinson appears in the index as Bishop of Southwark and in the text as suffragan bishop of Southwark. There is no such person, and he was of course suffragan bishop of Woolwich. It is quite evident that a glaring error like that must have been made initially by Edward, well advanced in years and far too close to his subject to see the wood for the trees. But he was atrociously served by his copy-editor and proof-reader. Instead of Fisher's death appearing in the Index under Fisher it has a separate, one line, entry. Edward had become buried beneath an alleged 365 boxes of papers, manhandled over the years across Westminster bridge from the library at Lambeth Palace. His own copy is a heart-rending mass of corrections and amendments, possibly made in the hope that they would be taken on board in the event of a reprint, or a paperback edition. There is no doubt that Edward was badly let down by the lack of funding for a proper copy editor and proof reader.

Bishop David Say claims that Edward often told those who had supplied material, and memories of Fisher, 'that he hoped to consult us further, but he never did. Towards the end he obviously found that he had no time for further consultation. This was sad because it meant that he made mistakes that could easily have been rectified, especially in the chapters about Fisher's involvement in the ecumenical movement and about his relations with Rome.' It seems that Margaret Pawley, the widow of Canon Bernard Pawley, the distinguished Anglican Observer at the Vatican Council, told

Bishop Say that 'Edward's chapter about this is "full of howlers".' Oliver Tomkins, from 1958 to 1975 bishop of Bristol and for many years the leading Anglican on the World Council of Churches, 'sent Edward several pages of comment and suggestions ... These Edward promised would be borne in mind for the paperback edition. Sadly, this has never appeared, a consequence, I suspect, of the delay in publishing the original book.'² In this surmise, Bishop Say is almost certainly correct.

While designating Edward 'one of the most loveable of Anglicans in my day' Lord Runcie, in a letter to the author, was fairly harsh in his verdict on *Fisher*. 'A long trek through endless speaking and writing made him waffly at the end so that he bequeathed to us a Life of Fisher which was unworthy of him or his subject.'³ But warm praise came at the time from an impressive source. Canon Paul Welsby, author of a concise and lucid handbook *How the Church of England Works*,⁴ wrote to Edward to congratulate him on *Fisher*, and for some inexplicable reason, instead of simply retaining Welsby's original letter, Edward transposed its original contents in his own hand on to Selwyn Avenue, Richmond notepaper.

'I've just finished reading your biography of Geoffrey Fisher,' Canon Welsby wrote, 'and I feel that I must write to congratulate you on a magnificent piece of work - one which far surpasses the biographies of Ramsey, Temple and Lang and is comparable with Bell's life of Davidson. As you will be aware from my letter to the *Church Times* last year, I have been among the impatient ones, regretting the delay in publication. I have now changed my mind and, having read the book, agree with Robert Runcie's judgement that the delay enables a reassessment of Fisher and his achievements at a time when distance makes a proper perspective easier to achieve. This is why your book is so much more satisfactory and rounder in judgement than Owen Chadwick's (through no fault of the author) Ramsey. [Michael Ramsey had asked Dr Chadwick to write his official Life as quickly as possible before a perhaps less sympathetic author might do so; it appeared only two years after Ramsey's death, with scarcely a critical comment, Lady Ramsey still being alive.]

In his Foreword to the book, written when he was still archbishop, Robert Runcie had said, 'We owe Dr Carpenter a great debt for his monumental labours in writing the Life of Archbishop Fisher, in particular for giving us access to the remarkable range of Fisher's papers now deposited at Lambeth.' Lord Runcie would have been most unlikely to contribute other than a generous Foreword; but with the benefit of further consideration, and in view of the fact that by the year 2000, when he wrote to the author, Edward was dead, he obviously felt free to shift his ground somewhat. Paul Welsby (who had been ordained by Fisher in Canterbury Cathedral) had told Edward, 'You must have been daunted by the vast amount of material and I greatly admire the way you have coped with this.' He ended on a note that will strike a chord with many biographers. 'I hope,' he said, 'you are not feeling too bereaved for it must be very strange, having in a sense "lived with" a person for so many years, suddenly to find that he has gone!'

Michael Adie, bishop of Guildford, writing in his diocesan newspaper, thought 'This massive biography will go far towards re-establishing Fisher's reputation as a great Archbishop and a loveable man. It will not go all the way for the book contains too much trivial detail - flight times, the number of hours sleep, tedious bread-and-butter letters - and should have been pruned. But it is a great book about a great man.'

Writing in *Theology*, Sir Derek Pattinson said he thought that younger readers would have benefited from 'more information about particular, now forgotten, individuals and causes.' This point was picked up too by Eric Kemp, the bishop of Chichester, when he reviewed the book in *The Times Literary Supplement*. 'As an historical source *Archbishop Fisher* is flawed,' Dr Kemp pronounced, 'but the task of compressing the subject matter into one volume must have been enormous. In spite of its deficiencies, Edward Carpenter has managed this with considerable skill.'

On Edward's 80th birthday he and Lilian were invited to a party at the Deanery, and Edward was allocated a stall in the Quire. They seem not to have returned, although invited, to the annual One People Oration, but Edward was invited to preach at a memorial service and on two occasions to read a Lesson. Michael Mayne recalls him being robed and processing 'for at least half-a-dozen services, such as the memorial services for Lord Trend, the High Bailiff, for Canon Charles and for a former Organist, Douglas Guest ... He was also present at the dinner in the Jerusalem Chamber to mark the retirement of Reg Pullen.'[5] The question of a dean or bishop returning too frequently to his old territory is sometimes a sensitive one (David Jenkins was delighted when his predecessor as bishop of Durham, Michael Ramsey, retired to live almost outside the cathedral door). But Edward and Lilian were hurt not to be invited to either of the two formal annual dinners, on St Peter's Day and what is called the Audit Dinner, but it was the view of the new dean that invitations to former incumbents on occasions such as those were not customary - and that he did not expect to be invited back to dinners either.[6]

The year that saw the publication of *Fisher*, 1991, Edward took the funeral of the 2nd earl Attlee; it was his father who had set Edward on the road to preferment. In 1992 he gave a lecture on Caxton, in the course of which he recalled a car journey he had once made to Winchester, driven by his son David, and had taken with him, 'to stimulate my mind on the journey', a copy of Cicero's letters in an edition which had the Latin on one page and an English translation on the other. On 2 January 1992 he had been writing to Michael about financial affairs. 'I am enclosing the latest statement of the current account. Ought I to disgorge some of it - maybe to the deposit account or elsewhere?'

In the 1950s Edward's father had given him money invested in building societies; there was a balance in December 1954 of £3,500 in the Co-Op Building Society, £3,000 in February 1957 in the Abbey National. 'These were reasonable sums of money in those days,' Michael, generally regarded as the financial wizard of the family, has written, 'and I would think the interest (rather than capital) would have paid school fees. My father had no interest in money and made no effort to invest this money other than place it in the building society. In 1962 the balance on his Abbey National Account had grown to £5,000 and the year before he died (when I closed the account on his behalf) the balance on the same account was £5,433 - not very good investing considering inflation in the intervening period, although admittedly for part of that time he would have been withdrawing the interest. [At the time Michael closed his father's account Edward was no longer able to manage his own affairs.]

'When we were young, although we went to Westminster School, we always had the impression that there was not much money to spare. I wouldn't say my father was "careful with money" as that gives the impression that he gave it thought. I don't think money was particularly significant to him, but certainly he did not like spending it unnecessarily. I remember him saying that investing in stocks and shares was like gambling - with a rather disapproving tone. Funnily enough my grandfather clearly did not object to investing in stocks and shares, as he had several (eg Rio Tinto) when he died.'[7]

Edward had ceased to preach and was entering his last phase of normal old age before tragically descending into Alzheimer's. He dictated a letter to Paul on 8 November 1995 to thank him for a trip to see his old home, Velvines, in Addlestone. He told Paul, 'I never cease to admire the way you handle a car, which is in fact a great art and gives confidence to those who are benefiting from it. All my love,' and there then followed, in a painful scrawl, 'Dad. I will be writing to you soon apropos your future.'

Michael dates the onset of a deterioration in his father's mental health to 'say the last six or seven years of his life,' in other words to about 1991. 'This manifested itself initially more in his being forgetful, particularly with names, and repeating himself in conversation.' Forgetting names is common to us all, and it was not really until the end of 1996 that any serious problems were detectable. In November that year he was entertained by the family to a birthday dinner at the Oxford and Cambridge Club in Pall Mall, 'when he was still reasonably OK.' But by the time he returned to the Club for dinner on Lilian's birthday in February the following year he apparently talked rationally to Michael's eldest daughter but 'it was clear that he did not know who she was.' He began to display some of the classic and very distressing symptoms of Alzheimer's Disease, following Lilian round the house, continually fidgeting, unable to remain seated, fiddling with his keys, shouting out for Lilian in the night. It eventually became obvious that he was going to need constant care, and he went into a nursing home in Twickenham, where every day for a year he was faithfully visited by Paul, who at first had found it difficult to behave with compassion towards his father when, if only subconsciously, he began to realise he was going to lose him. Once Edward had become totally dependent on others, the role of supportive father and helpless son were very movingly transposed.

Among the poems Edward wrote as a young man, around the time of his engagement, there emerged after his death an apparent and uncanny foretelling of his own bleak end:

> I have a fear that I shall die alone
> Inarticulate, imprisoned within a demented mind
> With symbols criss cross, ill-assorted, light turned to shadow
> And an ache for dim remembered things.
>
> I have a dull pain, a penury of spirit, pulled, pressed,
> A pain that will not feel; a pain that freezes and thaws me,
> Taunts the mind with chaos, criss cross and goes on, on
> Till thought chases slumbers and makes substance shadow.

Mercifully, Edward contracted a chest infection, which hastened the end of what had become, as for all Alzheimer's sufferers, a protracted living death; almost totally blind, Edward had little comprehension of the world but had no wish to leave it. 'He didn't want to die,' Lilian recalls. 'But even Edward couldn't hold out for ever. We were all with him at the end. We sang to him and recited poetry. Suddenly he drew his knees up to his chest and gave a great shout, as if in anger.'

Within days of Edward's death letters began to flood in. 'Very sad as it is to know that he has in one sense left us,' a friend wrote from Long Hanborough in Oxfordshire, 'I cannot think of Edward without a great sense of warmth and happiness. We are all so much the better for having known him.' 'We both had enormous respect for the way he lived a Christian life in addition to preaching about it,' two medical practioners from north London wrote. From south-west London a grateful former parishioner linked, as did many of those who wrote, her gratitude to

Edward with her knowledge that he and Lilian had worked in partnership. 'I often remember Dr Carpenter and you as the most remarkable team, and had it not been for you and your late husband's infinite kindness, guidance & support [...] would not have been able to overcome her immense grief after her father's death.'

The Jewish leader, Lord Jakobovits, rather oddly signing his letter 'Heartily yours,' noted Edward's 'historic contributions to inter-religious understanding and co-operation.' A duty priest at the Abbey from Lincolnshire wrote, 'Royal Peculiars do strange things to some priests, and laity also, but Edward was always the man of God.' A neighbour in Richmond said she had 'much missed his sprightly presence in Selwyn Avenue. He was so friendly and cheerful.' A former Director of the London Tourist Board told Lilian he thought the present state of the Abbey - 'more beautiful than at any time in its history' - stood as testimony to his work. By this time stricken with Parkinson's Disease and unable to write himself, Jeremy Thorpe asked his wife Marian to assure Lilian that Edward was 'a good man, but also a great man.'

The Cardinal Archbishop of Westminster, Basil Hume, also assured Lilian that Edward had been a great man. The Chief Rabbi, Dr Jonathan Sacks, recorded that Edward 'was an example to all of us in the ways of tolerance and understanding.' Someone wrote to say, 'It has been one of the most cherished privileges of my life to know Edward.' 'I really loved Edward,' a man whose wife told Lilian he found it difficult to focus on sad and emotional happenings, wrote from Poole in Dorset. 'I have vivid memories of his great kindness to me during my own Westminster years,' David Edwards wrote from his retirement home in Winchester. 'Whenever we came to the Abbey we met with a warm and friendly reception,' Lord Coggan recalled. 'He did so much in making the Abbey a human & welcoming place.'

'For me he is numbered among the great Christians of our time,' a letter from Shamley Green in Surrey proclaimed. 'Our years together were very happy and inspiring for me and I will always treasure the memory,' a former Surveyor of the Fabric wrote. 'Every memory I have is filled with his kindness and warmth,' someone wrote from Bristol for whom Edward had once spoken as a character witness. A former Lord Mayor of Westminster remembered how 'his humanity and humour were ever present.' And a former secretary of the Methodist Conference recalled 'with gratitude his kindness and courtesy.' He thought that Edward 'represented the best in Anglicanism but also appreciated all that was good in other religious traditions.'

'Like everyone else who ever met Edward,' a school governor wrote, 'I felt that my life had been enhanced by the experience.' 'He was consistently benevolent and beneficent,' someone else recalled. One of his godsons said that Edward would always be remembered 'as someone who gave very sound advice without frills.' 'I was much impressed, amongst many other things, by his remarkable humility,' someone who had only met him occasionally remarked. Bishop Baker's wife wrote to say, 'John & I both feel *so* privileged that we were at the Abbey when he was Dean.' 'A visit to his study was always stimulating and unpredictable' a former Precentor remembered. 'Edward was indeed a much loved and very special person' somebody wrote from Hampshire. From Honiton in Dorset came a note of thanks for having 'benefited from his wisdom and kindness.'

Edward's funeral took place in Westminster Abbey on 4 September 1998. The Queen and the Duke of Edinburgh were represented by a Baroness in Waiting, Lady Farrington, and the Prince of Wales by Rear Admiral David Macey. The Archbishop of Canterbury was represented by the Bishop at Lambeth, and the Speaker by Mr Nicholas Bevan. The Deputy Lord Mayor of Westminster attended, as did Lord Runcie and Cardinal Hume, who walked from Archbishop's House carrying his own case. As he was robing, Bishop Knapp-Fisher said it could not have been easy for him to attend, at such short notice - nine days, in fact, Edward having died on 26 August. 'How could I fail to be here,' the Cardinal replied, 'when Edward was such a dear friend.'

The Duke of Norfolk, a Roman Catholic, led a distinguished body of laity, which included Attlee's daughter Lady Felicity Harwood. Already Edward's successor as dean, Michael Mayne, had retired, and the new dean, Dr Wesley Carr, read the Bidding: 'Gathered in this Collegiate Church which he served with such distinction for 34 years we come to give thanks for the life and ministry of Edward Carpenter, priest, scholar and friend of many. We praise God for Edward's erudition, wit, pastoral sensitivity and his concern for men and women of many faiths and diverse circumstances. Throughout his ministry he was surrounded by a loving and caring family; we pray for the assurance of God's continuing care for him and for them.'

Paul, summoning up considerable courage, surely, read the first Lesson, from Corinthians: 'If I speak in the tongues of men and of angels, and have not love, I am a noisy gong and a clanging cymbal...' And Lilian stepped forward to read from probably Edward's favourite poet, Shelley: three stanzas of *Prometheus Unbound.* In his address the sub-dean, Canon Anthony Harvey, made the point that those poets who cropped up as they so often did when Edward talked 'were not there just for embroidery or illustration; they were participants in the endlessly questing conversation taking place in his mind and which he had a unique gift of sharing with others - with prince or tradesman, introverted intellectual or uncomplicated supporter of Chelsea Football Club, indeed with anyone who crossed his path.' Later that day Edward was cremated, his ashes being interred, in a private ceremony, beneath the nave of the Abbey.

On 27 July 2000 a Memorial Stone to Edward was dedicated in the nave of the ancient building he had served so long and faithfully. It reads: Edward Carpenter 1910-1998. Canon 1951-1974. Dean 1974-1985. Fearless in the cause of truth. Scholar, reconciler, friend.

NOTES AND REFERENCES

One: *Craftsmen and Builders*
1. In an Introduction to his book *The Age of Reason* (Constable, 1960) Harold Nicolson writes, 'It would be unwise to give precise dates for the Age of Reason, although conventionally it is identified with the eighteenth century.' But he reminds his readers that Horace Walpole claimed that the Age of Reason began as early as 1657. Percy Bysshe Shelley lived from 1792 to 1822.
2. Bishop John Baker to the author, 25 August 2000.
3. Dr David Carpenter to the author, 8 July 2000.
4. Published by SPCK for the Church Historical Society.

Two: *In the Steps of Byron*
1. Letter from Bishop David Say to Lilian Carpenter, 12 September 1998.
2. Letter from the Reverend Tim Gosden to the author, 14 August 2000.
3. Woolley eventually became rector of St Mary's, West Chiltington in Sussex, where he is buried alongside another holder of the Victoria Cross, Major General Henry Foote. Woolley won his VC in Belgium in 1915, Foote, who was also awarded the DSO, at the battle of Gazala in 1942.
4. Thirteen years after Edward left Holy Trinity the church became home to the Society for Promoting Christian Knowledge. Founded in 1698, it is the oldest Church of England mission agency, and has become a major religious publishing house. In a letter to the secretary of the Parochial Church Council, dated 12 February 1954, the Bishop of London, William Wand, wrote from Fulham Palace to say, 'I am very glad to hear of the spirit in which the people of Holy Trinity have, at some personal sacrifice, accepted the plan that their church should become the Spiritual and Administrative Centre of SPCK. I am glad to think that such a plan would ensure the continued usefulness of Holy Trinity in the life of the Church for many years to come.' SPCK remains accommodated at Holy Trinity to this day.

Three: *Stanmore*
1. Allen Lane.
2. Memorandum from Gladys Whittaker, June 2000.
3. Quoted by Edward Carpenter in *Archbishop Fisher: His Life and Times* (The Canterbury Press Norwich, 1991).

4. F A Iremonger, *William Temple: His Life and Letters* (OUP, 1948).
5. Letter from Lady Felicity Harwood to the author, 14 June 2000.
6. Memorandum from Bishop Say to the author.

Four: *Canons Ancient and Modern*
1. *Westminster Abbey*, with David Gentleman (Weidenfeld & Nicolson, 1987).
2. Ibid.
3. This has erroneously been referred to in Abbey literature as the King's 'last public appearance.' His official engagements included inviting Winston Churchill to form an administration and installing Princess Elizabeth and the Duke of Edinburgh as Privy Councillors; he saw South Pacific at Drury Lane and was present at London Airport to see Princess Elizabeth and her husband off to East Africa.
4. *That Man Paul* (Longmans, Green).
5. Letter to the author, 17 June 2000.
6. See *And Their Works Do Follow Them; The Story of the North London Collegiate School 1850-2000* by Nigel Watson (James & James, 2000).
7. Letter from Professor Cox to the author, 26 June 2000.
8. Letter to the author, 31 August 1998.

Five: *Baked Beans on Toast*
1. Barrie and Rockliff (1962). The diocese of Guildford had been founded in 1927, and until the cathedral had been built it had a provost, a post held for nine years prior to the consecration of the new cathedral by Walter Boulton. When Macmillan declined to nominate him dean there was an avalanche of criticism.
2. Letter from Lady Sandford to the author, 11 June 2000.
3. Letter to the author, 12 June 2000.
4. Watkins. London and Dulverton.
5. Undated letter to the author. Bishop of Birmingham 1978-87.
6. Letter from Fr Campbell, SSJE to the author, 13 June 2000.
7. To the author, 8 July 2000.
8. Ibid.
9. Letter from Canon Harvey to the author, 22 July 2000.
10. Letter from the librarian to the author, 4 September 2000.
11. Quoted in *A Wider Vision: A History of the World Congress of Faiths* by Marcus Braybrooke (Oneworld Publications, Oxford, 1996).
12. Op cit.

13. 30 August 1998.
14. Hamlet, Act 5 scene 2.

Six: *An Enemy Hath Done This*
1. Phoenix House, 1957, ed W R Matthews and W M Atkins.
2. Hodder & Stoughton, 1965.
3. Canon James to the author, 12 June 2000.
4. Mr Clarke to the author, 20 June 2000.
5. Op cit.
6. See *Michael Ramsey: A Portrait* by Michael De-la-Noy (Collins, 1990).
7. Op cit.

Seven: *Mr Dean*
1. On the staff of Westminster Abbey 1970-78, when he left to become dean of Norwich.
2. Letter from Bishop John Baker to the author, 25 August 2000.
3. Window on Westminster: A Canon's Diary 1976-1987 (SCM Press, 1998).
4. Ibid.
5. 'This incident [Edward Carpenter's arrival at an evening party at St Paul's Cathedral on his bicycle and very late, with his trousers tucked into his socks] and others like it led to his being labelled eccentric. Certainly Edward's behaviour was sometimes unusual, even odd, but egocentric he most emphatically was not.' Bishop Edward Knapp-Fisher speaking in Westminster Abbey on 27 July 2000.
6. Letter from Dean Trevor Beeson to the author, 1 July 2000.
7. Letter to the author, 14 June 2000.
8. Letter from Dean Beeson to the author, 10 August 2000.
9. Diaries, Op cit.
10. Delusions of Grandeur (HarperCollins, 1993).
11. A Westminster School publication, the *Elizabethan*.
12. Beeson diaries, Op cit.
13. Ibid, 22 December 1977.
14. Weidenfeld & Nicolson, 1989.
15. Diary, ob cit, 14 June 1978.
16. Ibid, 1 May 1980.
17. Lord Runcie to the author, 31 May 2000.
18. Canon Luff to the author, 27 June 2000.
19. Diaries, ob cit, 23 February 1981.
20. Ibid, 4 July 1981.

21. In conversation with the author.
22. 9 March 1984.
23. *A House of Kings*, Op cit.

Eight: *Daddy is Relaxing*
1. Letter from Canon Richardson to the author, 3 November 2000.
2. Memorandum from Bishop Say to the author, February 2000, Op cit.
3. 31 May 2000, Op cit.
4. Church Information Office, 1985.
5. Michael Mayne to the author, 24 August 2000.
6. Ibid.
7. Whether one takes a moral attitude towards the matter or not, Edward was perfectly right; investing in stocks and shares is exactly like gambling.

The Modern Churchman
Edward Carpenter, Westminster

by Trevor Beeson

Edward Carpenter, who was at Westminster Abbey from 1951 to 1985, first as a canon then from 1974 onwards, as dean, was an erudite and engaging churchman of a sort no longer bred. He was in the mould of his most eminent Victorian predecessor, A. P. Stanley, whom he greatly admired — a scholarly historian, a man of liberal mind, an eloquent preacher, a reformer, a lover of people and, above all, one who shared Stanley's vision of the Abbey as 'a religious, national and liberal institution'.

His 23 years as a canon were, because of this, a time of much frustration. He was not unhappy, for he loved the Abbey, but he was for most of the time condemned to serve in ultra-conservative chapters in which new ideas were constantly rejected. Thus when he became dean, at the age of 64, he was very much 'an old man in a hurry' and effected more changes in the Abbey's day-to-day life than any of his predecessors since Stanley. Exempt from compulsory retirement, he stayed until he was 75 and remained convinced that continuity required constant reformation.

Most of the old formalities that gave the impression of stuffiness were dispensed with and visitors, whether attending a service or simply passing through on a guided tour, were more warmly welcomed - often by the dean himself. This was not always easy, as the advent of wide-bodied jet aircraft in the 1970s sometimes led to the Abbey being overwhelmed by overseas tourists. An American who had been nearly trampled to death, then found his pocket picked, took some convincing that a pilgrimage to the shrine of Edward the Confessor was 'a spiritual experience'. But the dean tried.

A lifelong pacifist, Carpenter believed that the Commonwealth, together with the United Nations, was a vital instrument of peace, so the High Commissioners in London were invited to read a lesson at evensong on their national independence days, and attend a social gathering afterwards. A high point in his year was the annual Commonwealth Day Observance attended by the Queen, the High Commissioners and their staffs, and conducted by the leaders of all the main religious faiths.

Inter-faith relations was another high priority which took him into active membership of the Council of Christians and Jews. The Dalai Lama was accorded greater loyalty than most Christian leaders and this sometimes led to problems. Members of the chapter were surprised to learn from a Sunday newspaper that the heavily guarded Tibetan leader would not only be staying at the deanery but also give Buddhist teaching in depth in the Abbey. In the event he spoke about peace. The strictly vegetarian deanery household was thrown into a turmoil when His Holiness required bacon, liver and sausages for breakfast.

Although Carpenter had a first-class mind and rarely considered a matter without reference to its history, he was essentially a romantic and an idealist. This often led him to look upon life with an almost child-like simplicity. The fact of sin and the necessity of compromise were for him almost too painful to contemplate; the Sermon on the Mount provided the ethical basis for political as well as personal conduct. Cruelty in the natural order also greatly troubled him and he was active in animal welfare societies.

His theological outlook was shaped by the early twentieth-century Modernist movement, which viewed much of the Bible and most traditional Christian doctrine with a marked degree of scepticism. He remained a leading member of the Modern Churchmen's Union long after its post-1939-45 war decline. This gave him a certain affinity and a good deal of sympathy with the *Honest to God* radicalism of the 1960s but, inasmuch as he had been largely unaffected by the Biblical Theology and Liturgical Movements, his position was different and he became something of a 'period piece'.

A fine, albeit somewhat prolix, preacher, he rarely referred to the Bible in his sermons and often selected a text from Cicero or Plato and illustrated his points with copious quotations from his beloved Shelley or the almost equally revered Dr Johnson. Poetry was always very important to him and during his time as dean 11 memorials were added to Poet's Corner — as many as in the previous 250 years. He also felt free to replace bloodthirsty and obscure Old Testament lessons with something he believed to be more edifying, and on more than one occasion prefaced the reading of a New Testament lesson with the comment 'St Paul got things wrong'.

In constant demand for sermons elsewhere and always ready to accept invitations — he loved rail travel — asking him to preach involved certain hazards. His diary was not always well ordered, leaving him booked to be in the pulpit of different churches at the same time. Or he might lose his way while walking from the station and arrive breathless long after the service had started, with the vicar in despair. Having arrived, his sermon could be quite unrelated to the subject on which he had been asked to speak, but would be recognized as a tour de force delivered by a man whom it was a delight to meet over a cup of coffee afterwards.

Carpenter's unpredictability and informality made his relations with the royal family less easy than the close friendships enjoyed by his immediate predecessor, Eric Abbott, and certainly by Dean Stanley whose wife was a lady-in-waiting at the Court. He was never invited to lunch at Buckingham Palace and this, not because he was unappreciated but probably because he did not quite conform to royal expectations. Entirely unselfconscious, he treated everyone alike and on those occasions when duty took him to Buckingham Palace for some function he would weave his way through the London traffic on his ancient bicycle, clad in a shabby suit and coloured scarf, and on arrival forget that his trousers were tucked into his socks. In conversation he could seem abstracted and abruptly depart from the subject under discussion. When the dean and chapter entertained Queen Elizabeth, the Queen Mother, on the occasion of her eightieth birthday, the dean proposed her health with moving eloquence but then absent-mindedly seized her carefully prepared gin and tonic and downed it himself. Her Majesty was greatly amused and the dean was in no way disconcerted. The decision of the Prince of Wales to have his ill-fated marriage in St Paul's (made for architectural reasons) was a deep disappointment to him, not because he desired the limelight — he was much too humble for that — but because it seemed to be a denial of the Abbey's historic role.

Edward Frederick Carpenter, the son of a local builder of modest means, was born in 1910 at Addlestone, near Weybridge. He went from Strodes School, Egham, to King's College, London, where he took a first in history, followed by an MA with distinction and later a PhD. His chief interest at this time was in late seventeenth- and early eighteenth-century Anglicanism and he wrote biographies of Bishop Thomas Sherlock, Archbishop Thomas Tennison and Bishop Henry Compton. While at King's he came under the influence of liberal theology and transferred to the theological faculty to prepare for ordination.

He was a curate at Holy Trinity, Marylebone, from 1935 to 1941 and while there met and married Lilian Wright, a student at the Royal Academy of Dramatic Art, who played a vital part in his future ministry and eventually introduced him to the Baha'i faith. After a further curacy at St Paul's, Harrow, he was appointed vicar of Great Stanmore, Middlesex. There he had six idyllic years, relishing every aspect of the work of a parish priest and making an impact that was remembered half a century later by those who had been his young parishioners. Among those who were impressed was the then Prime Minister, C.R. Attlee, who had a house in Stanmore, and in 1951 he took the opportunity to appoint

Carpenter to a vacant canonry of Westminster.

This was not a popular move at the Abbey. He was young, he had been to a redbrick university, and undoubtedly he was a Socialist. Attlee had totally disregarded ecclesiastical advice. Carpenter's early years in the Little Cloister were not easy. For a time he was cold-shouldered, and there seemed nothing for him to do, but eventually his own warm humanity melted the hearts of his colleagues and he found his feet. The fact that he had time on his hands meant that he was able to pursue his studies and write books. He also became involved in a great number of liberal movements and organizations, joining forces with his friend John Collins, of St Paul's, in the campaign for the abolition of capital punishment, the campaign for nuclear disarmament, and the anti-apartheid movement.

He was present at the Coronation in 1953 and carried to the altar the orb — a prophetic symbol, perhaps, of his own future global concerns. There was a young family to bring up and he and Lilian delighted to keep open house: so open that once when returning from an early morning service in the Abbey he met two stocking-footed burglars leaving by his front door and, either innocently or absent-mindedly, expressed the hope that they had had a good night. In 1959 he was, in the absence of any other willing candidate, appointed treasurer of the Abbey and held this post for 15 years until he became dean. It was not an office for which he was temperamentally suited, but he carried it off by getting the Receiver General, who ran administration, to hand him the accounts and budgets at the beginning of chapter meetings. These, although previously unseen, he presented with the aplomb and apparent expertise of a high-powered financier, leaving the Receiver General to field any questions.

The office of archdeacon, to which he was elected in 1963, was much more to his liking, and this, not simply because it was essentially a sinecure, but because it gave him a pastoral relationship with the 26 parishes of which the dean and chapter were the Patrons. He greatly enjoyed visiting them, preaching, encouraging their clergy and musing on their historic links with the Abbey. Later, when he became dean, they were invited to Westminster for half a day — for a tour of the Abbey, tea and evensong. The parish priests were encouraged to come more frequently and to spend the inside of a week in the precincts, while responsible for hourly prayers in the Abbey.

Having been appointed to Westminster when only 41, it was natural that he should sometimes wonder if the remainder of his life was to be spent in the service of the Royal Peculiar or if he might be asked to move elsewhere. With the right kind of administrative support, he would have made an exciting bishop and become a much-loved pastor of a diocese. Succession to Bishop Barnes at Birmingham would have been an imaginative choice by the Crown, but the route to the episcopate was barred by Archbishop Geoffrey Fisher, as Carpenter discovered when undertaking research for Fisher's biography. Among the papers at Lambeth was a copy of a letter from the Primate to the Prime Minister in which he advised that under no circumstances should Canon Edward Carpenter be preferred to a bishopric, since he was interested in many things and ought to become a professor of history.

When the rectory of St Margaret's, Westminster, which is annexed to a canonry of Westminster, fell vacant in 1956 Carpenter asked if he might be considered for transfer to this post. He would have been an ideal choice and taken seriously the preaching opportunities and the church's link with the House of Commons, but the dean, Alan Don, told him in the nicest possible way that a Socialist could not be appointed to so fashionable a church. A quarter of a century later, when St Margaret's was facing bankruptcy and closure, Treasurer Carpenter, whose affection for the church never wavered, came to the rescue with the proposal that it should be reincorporated into the Abbey, from which it had been separated in 1837. He was much involved in the drafting of a Parliamentary Bill to make this possible.

His disappointment over St Margaret's was, however, as nothing compared with the anguish he felt over his failure to be appointed Dean of St Paul's in 1967. Carpenter was in no sense an ambitious man, but the deanery of St Paul's was the one post in the Church of England, outside Westminster, in which he believed he could make a significant contribution. Moreover, the retiring dean, W.R. Matthews, had written to him expressing the hope that he would be his successor and indicating that he would recommend him to the Crown. The only other serious candidate seemed to be John Collins, who was senior canon of St Paul's, and the two friends would have been content if either had been appointed. But in the event Martin Sullivan, the junior canon, was chosen and, since his gifts were largely confined to after-dinner speaking, insult was added to injury. Both Carpenter and Collins were devastated and for the next 11 years St Paul's had totally inadequate leadership.

Meanwhile, the Abbey community was still recovering from the strenuous celebration of the 900th anniversary of its foundation by King Edward the Confessor in 1065. Three members of the chapter (Eric Abbott, Max Warren and Joost de Blank) were invalids, another (Michael Stancliffe) was rector of St Margaret's, so it was left to Carpenter to plan and implement a programme. Which he did with gusto, crowding in as many events as 365 days could carry. A great variety of people were drawn into the Abbey's life and the celebration was deemed to have been a huge success, but everyone, apart from Carpenter, was left exhausted. He also managed to edit a large new history of the Abbey, *A House of Kings,* which remains an invaluable resource for both the scholar and the general reader.

When Eric Abbott, who had been ill for several years, retired in 1974 the Chapter made strong representations to the Crown that Carpenter should be his successor. No one knew more about the Abbey or embodied its spirit more than he, and it was hard to believe that any other priest in the Church of England was better equipped for this special post. The Labour Prime Minister, Harold Wilson, had no difficulty in concurring and indeed attended the installation, though the length of the new dean's sermon required him to leave early to deal with urgent matters in the House of Commons. Thus began an 11-year reign that proved to be a happy experience for everyone involved in the Abbey's life and a fitting climax to an outstanding ministry.

Inevitably perhaps, his love for people and sheer goodness proved to be a disability when he was called upon to administer discipline. It was too easy to take advantage of his incapacity to recognize sin and he sometimes tolerated conduct that ought not to have been tolerated. But the open house deanery and the sight of the dean bustling about the cloisters or risking his life (he had very impaired sight) by cycling across Westminster and the West End to visit someone who was ill exuded goodwill. It even made it possible to forgive a 4 a.m. telephone call from California, made by a dean who was apparently unaware that clock time in London was different.

Carpenter could himself manage on very little sleep and, having simply added his decanal responsibilities to the multitude of commitments he had accumulated over the previous 23 years, it was hardly surprising that he could never turn to the writing of a book much before midnight. During his time as a canon he had published several books, the most substantial of which *Cantuar* (1971) — was a valuable compilation of brief lives of all the Archbishops of Canterbury. Then, shortly before moving to the deanery, he undertook to write the official biography of Archbishop Geoffrey Fisher. This was a strange alliance, since he had little in common with Fisher and had often been highly critical of his Primacy, but as he became immured in the task he developed a liking for his subject, amounting almost to admiration, and became so fascinated with Fisher's life and times that he found it impossible to lay it down. He took it with him into retirement and 19 years after signing the original publisher's contract, the 820-page volume was permitted to see the light of day. It was more in the expansive style of a Victorian biography than of an analytical modern study but will always be an important quarry of twentieth-century Church history.

Dean Stanley spent much of his time at Westminster exploring and documenting the royal vaults and in 1977 Carpenter was given the opportunity to follow modestly in his somewhat macabre footsteps. The smell of gas in proximity to the Stuart vault caused anxiety lest an escape from the public supply was accumulating and threatening an explosion. There had recently been disastrous instances of this in some blocks of flats. Royal permission to open the vault was obtained and late on a quiet evening in July the dean and chapter and a few historians descended into the cellar-like room to view the scene described by Stanley — the lead coffins of King William III and Queen Mary, of Orange, and of Queen Anne and her consort, Prince George of Denmark, intact but that of Charles II caved in and revealing the decayed remains of the once 'Merry Monarch'. Carpenter, the historian, was deeply moved and returned immediately to pen an account of what some others had experienced as a disturbing event. There was no gas.

During his latter years as treasurer and throughout his time as dean, the Abbey and St Margaret's church underwent major restorations that transformed their exteriors, leaving them gleaming white as if newly built. The original appeal for £5 million had to be doubled and eventually raised to £20 million. This was efficiently handled by the Duke of Edinburgh and a sequence of city magnates, without much effort from the canons. But the dean was required to present the Abbey's public face at a multitude of fundraising occasions, where his enthusiasm and evident commitment had a powerful influence.

Following his retirement in 1985 he remained active, retaining his links with liberal causes and continuing to deliver erudite sermons and speeches. His lifelong support of Chelsea Football Club was reflected by the football included in his official coat of arms. By the time death liberated him from the sad indignities of Alzheimer's disease in 1998 he had lived through the greater part of the most turbulent and dangerous century in human history. And the dean of unorthodox faith had always been a beacon of hope and love.

Selections from The Old Boys' Network:
A Headmaster's Diaries 1972 – 1986

by John Rae

These selections from the diaries of the late John Rae, Headmaster of Westminster School 1970 – 1986, cover Edward's appointment as Dean and the service in Westminster Abbey following the appointment of Dom Basil Hume as Roman Catholic Archbishop of Westminster.

21 December 1973

David Carey telephones to discuss our approach to Colin Peterson, the prime minister's appointments secretary, about who the school would like to see as the new dean when Eric Abbot retires. David is legal secretary to the archbishop of Canterbury and a governor of the school. He is devoted to the school but he is an intriguer who likes to be the king-maker, the man behind the scenes who influences key appointments. I want Edward Carpenter to be the new dean but Carey will have his own candidate.

11 January 1974

See Reg Pullen [Receiver General] … We talk about the dean's retirement and his possible successor. Reg has already seen Colin Peterson and gives the impression that he has urged Edward Carpenter's candidature but he warns that Edward will be ruled out because the Establishment fears he will let his political and ethical convictions influence his actions as dean; that if Bomber Harris dies and approaches are made for an Abbey burial, Edward would object on pacifist grounds.

This evening, I go round to Little Cloister to see Edward and it is soon clear that he has some hopes of the deanery. He would be so good and the appointment would be a reward for a brave and intelligent man. Of course, I have a selfish reason for wanting Edward to be dean and ex-officio chairman of the governors; it would strengthen my hand vis-à-vis the governing body. But I fear the establishment will play safe and dull.

14 January 1974

I see David Carey about our visit to Colin Peterson on Wednesday. Carey is open about his tactics: he will argue against Edward Carpenter (too Liberal), suggest Bishop Geoffrey Tiarks (who he thinks would not accept), leaving the field open for his real candidate, the bishop of Ely.

16 January 1974

At 4pm, David Carey and I walk to No 10 to see Colin Peterson. It is an interesting meeting. Peterson says very little; he listens and makes notes. I tell him what the school wants in a new dean: the ability to lead the governing body and an interest in the school. Then I cannot resist adding a pastoral gift for bringing warmth and Christian love to the whole Abbey community, which has lacked these qualities for so long.

20 January 1974

I pay a call on the dean [Eric Abbott] this evening and he talks openly about who he would like to succeed him. He would like Owen Chadwick from Cambridge and failing that, Michael Stancliffe, the dean of Winchester. No mention of Edward Carpenter. I suspect the dean has timed his resignation while there is a Tory prime minister to ensure Edward does not get the job.

24 January 1974

At 3.30pm, to Lambeth Palace to see Archbishop Ramsey about the dean's successor. As it happens, I have 10 minutes first with Bishop Geoffrey Tiarks, the archbishop's senior chaplain, who has been strongly tipped for the job. Our discussion is on two levels. We talk about the school's hopes of the new dean but we both know that we may soon have to get on as headmaster and chairman of the governors. He asks my opinion of Edward Carpenter, presumably to find out how close I am to Edward. He then says he thinks Edward may be 'a little unstable' and I correct him ... At last I see the archbishop and spend a few minutes explaining why the choice of dean is so important for the school. He listens and asks a few questions and then I depart.

17 April 1974

I am discussing the budget and fees for 1974/5 with the bursar and Vic Shannon, the accountant, when the telephone rings. It is Edward Carpenter who says simply, 'The age of miracles has not passed'. I understand at once what he means and I am overjoyed but I replace the receiver and continue with the financial discussion. The news is confidential until next week. Later Daphne and I go round to Little Cloister to see Edward and Lilian to congratulate them and to express our delight that Edward is going to be the next dean. Edward shows me Harold Wilson's letter; it came by hand, an envelope within an envelope, 'My dear archdeacon'. It is marvellous news. I did not give Edward much chance because the Church establishment was against him, but the arrival of Wilson at No.10 made all the difference. [Edward Heath, the Conservative prime minister, called a general election for 28 February, following which Harold Wilson became prime minister of a minority Labour government.] For the school, it is an appointment of the greatest significance and it is for my future too; to work with Edward as the chairman of the governors is a pleasure I never thought to enjoy.

21 March 1976

I attend a very special occasion in the Abbey. Edward Carpenter, the dean, has invited the new Roman Catholic Archbishop of Westminster, Dom Basil Hume of Ampleforth, and Benedictine monks from all over England to sing vespers in the Abbey. The Abbey is packed for the first time in goodness knows how many years and 150 Benedictine monks sing vespers in what was once their monastic church for the first time since the Reformation. Edward introduces the archbishop and Basil Hume responds, at which the congregation bursts into applause. There is applause again when dean and archbishop walk out together through the choir and down the nave. It is altogether a very remarkable, historic occasion, and I cannot help thinking that no other dean would have allowed such an ecumenical service to be held in the Abbey.

18 May 1979

Lunch with Harold Wilson and Marcia at the Athenaeum [Wilson had resigned as Prime Minister on 5 April 1976] … I ask him about his choice of Edward Carpenter as dean of Westminster, and he replies that even before he won the election, he was determined to appoint Edward and had no difficulty imposing his choice on the appointments secretary at No. 10.

28 December 1980

We dine with David and Patsy Puttnam. Harold Wilson is also a guest. He has recovered from an operation but still looks weak and suffers from short-term memory loss. However his grasp of historical detail is as extraordinary as ever ... When I tell him that one of the best things he did when he was prime minister was to appoint Edward Carpenter dean of Westminster, he can recall every stage of his battle with the Church of England establishment. There was, he says, a powerful anti-Carpenter lobby orchestrated by the man in Downing street responsible for advising on Church appointments, but Harold favoured Carpenter and so - according to Harold - did the Queen, although officially she was not allowed to express an opinion. The church lobby fought very hard to block Carpenter but the Prime Minister had the last word.

Glimpses of a London Childhood

by Lilian Carpenter

I was born at Number 138, Great Titchfield Street. This street was built in the 18th Century for fairly well-off families. It was part of the Portland Estate. I was born in February in the year 1917. My family lived in just two rooms below-stairs, which were originally the cook's quarters in those days. The gate in the railings indicated where there had been a flight of steps leading down to the rooms below; these were used in the olden days by the tradesmen. However by the time we occupied them the steps had been removed. The house was now divided up into various flats and 32 people were living there. We all used the same front door which had to be left open.

My family was Mum, Dad, Alice, Ted, myself, Marge, Bob and Joan and we all lived in just two rooms. There was a front room which had a long passage-way at the side leading to the area where the coal holes were under the pavement. Through the front window we could look up to the railings and see the legs of people passing by. The back room, our living room and also our parents' bedroom, had one window opening on to a yard and there was an outhouse where there was a large stone sink with a cold water tap and where we all had to go for all our water. The lavatory was at the end of this yard and had to be shared by three families. This outside lavatory had a large wooden seat and there was a long handled chain. There was always plenty of torn up newspapers there for wiping our bottoms. The couple who lived in the back parlour used a bucket and when it needed emptying the man who was a cripple would bring their bucket down the stairs to empty it. I still remember how indescribably awful the smell was and how some of it used to slop onto the stairs.

Living there, starting from the top of the house was Mrs Ball, a widow, who had a grown up son and daughter who occasionally visited her. Nearly every day I would be asked to get her a pennyworth of milk. I always enjoyed this errand because it gave me the opportunity and great thrill to look out of her window. I would fancy I was the Queen looking out on my subjects. Below her was a quiet Jewish family, who were always kind to us. Underneath her was a large vociferous family who owned a stall in the market. We were sometimes given a large pan of sweetened damsons by them. Occasionally there was trouble in the house and we would hear quarrelling and shouting and then sometimes following this we heard the running of footsteps and the slamming of the front door. I always found this frightening. On the first floor, in the front room lived a blind man with his deaf wife and grown-up daughter who was slightly disabled but intelligent. Their granddaughter had lost both parents with tuberculosis and the grandparents brought her up with them. At the back parlour was the crippled man with his wife. At the front on the ground floor lived a quiet Jewish couple who kept to themselves. When the door was open I sometimes peeped in and saw everything so neat, clean and tidy.

And then there was our family, the Wright family, occupying the kitchens. A flight of stairs led down to our domain; there were no lights so in the winter it was very dark.

Living so close to other families we of course became involved in their lives. I used to hear snatches of conversation just as I passed; grown-ups were talking either on the steps, stairs or in the shops. Mums used to come out just before the sun set for a little fresh air and stand on their steps and enjoy together a little gossip. I did errands for a number of people: Mrs Ball at the top of our house and the Jewish couple who gave me something to eat as I was always hungry. I shopped daily for a sad couple who lived in kitchens like us only six houses along Great Titchfield Street. The husband was very tall and rather bent; he was a shoemaker for a firm a little way off. His wife was an invalid with a very crippling disease. She could hardly hobble around but her mind was clear and very lucid. I would earn a threepenny piece from her. I remember their kitchen. It was one of my very early memories. I must have been just a toddler, left with a very old deaf lady. My mother had gone off to do a cleaning job. In my mind I can still see so clearly the mat that I was sat on: it was black, with long matted edges. I was given a large bag of peanuts and sat in front of the fire. I cannot say what my thoughts were but I must have been quite small. The old lady had a large black cat that just sat and looked at me; it seemed such a long time that I was left sitting there. I believe I cried a lot. Everything seemed to me to be so very dark and gloomy, except for the fire – even the cat, the rug and the old lady.

Although we lived in close proximity to so many families in our house, we somehow managed in a way to keep aloof though I knew that to the other families we were "That Wright family who are so poor."

My mother would hang the washing up in the back yard and on a hot summer's day we could have our window open and I could glimpse the blue sky. Sometimes the drains would get blocked and my mother would take up the large cover and throw buckets of water down until all became clear again. When I looked down I thought how very strange the shapes were inside the drain. There was a covered place at the back where the washing was done and there stood several mangles. The one my mother used was a fairly respectable one. She used to take in mangling and I had to deliver it getting the three pennies or sixpence that my mother charged. As I grew older I used to plan how these areas could be used to better advantage for us children. It was in this open area that Eve and I would give concerts; the entrance fee was a halfpenny for which they got not only an entertainment, but also a cup of lemonade made with lemonade powder, and half a stale bun. On one occasion I borrowed my elder brother's first pair of long trousers to perform 'O Captain my Captain'. For this misdemeanour I got a slap around the face. Eve and I also did all the fairy scenes from A Midsummer Night's Dream. She was always the Fairy and I was always Puck. There were stairs in the area which led to a coal cellar. Sometimes it contained a bag of coal but sometimes only a lot of rubbish.

The security of our two rooms, being my home, meant a great deal to me. Because our front door was always unlocked, anyone from outside could get in. This often worried me if I was alone. We only had in the front room where we girls slept a small wooden catch which we could use. Sometimes when I came home from school and found my mother had scrubbed the kitchen table or washed over the lino it made me so very happy. My parents' room was also the room for eating and for the preparation of food. A large table stood in front of the large bed which we used to sit on at meal times. There was also a gas stove and oven, a fireplace, a corner cupboard where we should have kept our food, and a cupboard under the window. My mum and dad slept in the big bed. There was a little truckle bed where my two brothers slept and we girls slept in the front room.

The Neighbourhood

Great Titchfield Street was part of the Portland Estate and it wasn't until I saw our street years later marked on an old map that I realised that the Wright family, along with all the other families, occupied rooms once reserved for kitchens. We could look along Bolsover Street to the end where our church, Holy Trinity Marylebone, then stood. It stands in Marylebone Road and now faces Great Portland Street station, which was not there then. It was a fine building and we felt always that it belonged to us. Round about Christmas time we would wander to Oxford Street and look at the windows filled with toys and other wonderful things. We would spread out our arms across the window and say: "These are all mine!" One day a kind lady invited us in and bought us a present. I am afraid that I can't remember what it was, because in my imagination, everything was mine.

Running parallel to Great Titchfield Street, but behind, was Charlton Street. One end was known for its bad characters. My friend Eve's Aunt lived here and sometimes we would have to deliver a message so we would venture down it. It was also the way to our Brownies and to Sunday School classes which were held in a school building. When we were Guides we would stand at the bus stop with our beloved guide captain, Dorothy Sayers, and wait for her 25 bus to Cricklewood.

A great division, Great Portland Street, ran right across our parish, one side with very poor families and the other side with very well off doctors, other professionals and very rich residents. This was peculiar to our parish and unlike most others.

On bank holidays we would venture outside our domain and walk all the way to Hampstead Heath to the fair which was held there every bank holiday. We only had a few pennies between us, but once we asked a man if he could win a coconut for us, and he did! By the time we arrived home we had eaten it all! It was such a long walk from Hampstead Heath and we had to walk home as we had no money for the bus. We were so very tired but the coconut had helped!

A favourite walk was to Regent's Park ... our Mecca! From an early age I loved all beautiful things, especially flowers. So on many occasions we would go with a party of the Great Titchfield Street Kids to the park. Our mother would give us some jam sandwiches wrapped up in newspaper and also a bottle of tea. We would always push a pram of some sort. Often the bread and tea were consumed before ever we reached the park! When we got there we would settle down by the swings and the sand pit and stay there until dusk. When Eve and I went on our own we had favourite places: we would choose between our 'May Tree Home' and our 'Elm Tree Home'. We were always very put out if they were already occupied. In this wonderful evergreen haven I learnt to appreciate the birds and especially the song of the blackbird which would often be singing as we made our way homewards – tired, grubby but very happy children.

Some days we would walk the length of the Broad Walk and across the grass until we reached the zoo. In those days we had a free view of many of the animals in their open compounds. One day we walked to Primrose Hill, but were very disappointed not to find any primroses; however we had a lovely roll down the hill. When we became old enough for Guides, after parade we would go for a cherished walk with our beloved and very much adored Captain and other officers. With her we learned a great deal about trees and their uses. This knowledge I treasured and was able to pass on to my patrol when I became a Patrol Leader. We were so very fortunate to have almost on our doorstep such a wonderful expanse of verdant land. Eve and I would go in the summer to the park for a swing. So you see in this vicinity, my school, my Church and the park all played a very large part in the formation of my character.

My favourite shop sold a loaf called Neville's; it had a small bun shape on the top with a large oval beneath. The texture of this Neville's bread was delicious. When my mother could afford a loaf I asked for the crust. As we all wanted the crust it was often a wrangle over which one of us got it. Then the greatest treat was a slice of bread and dripping. Sometimes I would accompany a friend to a Welsh dairy to get an ounce of butter. I would so enjoy watching the woman, meticulously dressed in white, take a wooden platter in each hand, and in a minute manipulate a piece of golden butter from their huge block, work on it until the one ounce looked like a piece of pure gold. This was transferred onto a small piece of paper and she then made it into a little parcel. At home we never had butter because we could not afford it; however one day my elder sister eventually bought us a whole quarter of a pound as a treat for us all. I remember watching with amazement in this same dairy, businessmen having two eggs whipped up in a glass of milk for their lunch. Fancy having two eggs!

A few shops before the dairy was the oil shop. This was a most valuable shop for people who were poor like us. Here one could get anything from soap to a can of oil. I was often sent there for a pennyworth of vinegar or some hard brown soap for my mother's washing. It had a disturbing smell that thrilled and absorbed me. Two great chaps ran the oil shop; one was short and sturdy and called George and the other man was tall and good looking. Sometimes George would give me a sweet from a wooden box that they kept on the counter. This was a very great treat. They were expensive creams, of soft shades of pink, white and lavender and were delicious and melted in my mouth. I could never really understand why sweets were in an oil shop. How very sad I was to hear that during the war this little row of shops had all been bombed and destroyed and the two men had been killed.

We had a public house on each corner; I remember that Finches was the name of one and here men would drown their sorrows and spend their wages that should have gone to feed their family. Often I've seen children late at night sitting outside waiting for their parents to come home. My mother never went into the Public Bar because of gossiping neighbours. She went to a little side entrance or she would send us in there with a little jug to have it filled with ale. In winter she would put a red hot poker into it to make mulled ale.

Frumkin's was the sweet shop on the corner run by a Jewish family. The Grandmother sat in the shop but she couldn't speak any English. Whenever we had a halfpenny to spend we went to this sweet shop where we children spent endless moments deciding what we should buy. Sometimes it was a blackjack which lasted a very long time and then there was Spanish Braid, long liquorice strips; there were also gobstoppers which when you sucked them changed into wonderful colours. Sometimes we sucked one colour and let a friend have a suck on the next colour before demanding it back. There were so many delights from which we made our choice. We could even get a few sweets for a farthing!

Another shop in the market was the butcher's. I would be sent to get a pennyworth of bones and then on to the greengrocer's stall for a pennyworth of pot herbs. We would get an onion, two swedes, a turnip and a carrot. My mother would make a big stew of these and after boiling everything together would pop in some dumplings to fill us all up. I never liked having to go to the butcher's shop. To me it was the ugliest in the street for several whole skinned animals would hang outside the shop, and blood would drip down onto sawdust. To me it was a pitiful sight.

A very valuable shop, for poor people who could not afford to go to the doctor, was the chemist shop. My mother, when we had coughs and colds, would send me to the chemist on the corner of Cleveland Street. I had to memorise about five or six different ingredients. I would run all the way muttering to myself, "syrup of squills, ippipecuanna wine" and so on. This usually remedied our coughs or colds together with a good rub of our chests with the camphorated oil and this would soon see the end of our trouble. I loved the window of the chemist because there were large pear-shaped glass bottles full of coloured liquid. I would look at these for ages.

The shop I liked even better was in Cleveland Street. This was Solly's fish and chip shop. My mother would often say: "You're not like the kids up the street who get nothing but fish and chips every day." Then of course I would think how much I would like to be one of them and even just have the chips. I was often hungry. When I was older and coming home from Guides my friends would be able to buy a pennyworth of chips with salt and vinegar on them; they always shared with me. I sometimes went with Eve when her family were having a fish dinner. She would always ask for plenty of crackling. Crackling was a free extra as it was the fried bits of broken off fish and these she would always give to me.

How did the very poor manage? Some finally had to go into the workhouse where families were separated. Elderly couples who had never been apart were forced to end their days, the men with men and women in the women's section. Others, a little better off, had the indignity of being 'on the parish'. This meant a little money brought by a parish worker to help tide them over. To help ourselves we would have to get things for nothing or very cheaply. I can recall having to get up very early on a cold winter morning and being sent on a long walk to the end of Great Titchfield Street into Oxford Street where there was a very exclusive bread and cake shop called Buzzards. Here they would give me some stale bread. I would take an old pillow case to take as much as they would give. My sister would be sent to queue at Craddocks in Westminster, a long walk away, for cracked eggs and giblets. On some Fridays my mother would walk all the way to The Cut near Waterloo Station to get some very cheap fish.

Another market near us was in Seaton St just off the Euston Road. Late on Saturday the vendors would sell off meat and vegetables very cheaply. On some Sundays there were special occasions when my Mother would go to the market early to get a cheap joint. Sunday lunch was generally a bit better than week days. I wouldn't say that my mother was a good cook, but she managed to keep us all alive. I am afraid that when I went into other people's houses I would think: "If only this could be my home and this could be my mother."

My Father and my Mother

My father always wore a stiff white collar and would often find it difficult to put two studs in, one at the back and one in the front. He was very short sighted and had to wear thick glasses. He had fine hands although when I saw them they were usually covered with grease or dye or wax as his work was shoe mending.

Whenever he had been drinking too much, out would come his mouth organ. He was a superb master of the instrument and could play tune after tune without pausing, then he would have to stop to get the saliva out of the instrument, by banging it on his hand, before starting again. All would be well until he played 'Mother I love you', and then he would break down. His mother died when he was young and he was brought up by his older sisters. He was the last to be born of a second marriage and lived in Fisher Street, WC1. We children hated the mouth organ because it often made him cry. He had several mouth organs which he kept in their colourful boxes. He was obviously musical but without training.

I remember going to stay with his sister in East Ham. It was around Christmas time. I remember that I refused to go up the stairs to bed so I slept on the settee. The front door opened into this room and in what seemed to me to be the middle of the night, a policeman came in and took off his helmet and was given a drink.

My father was strong and well built. When we were young he would throw us up into the air and catch us. He had such a warm and kindly smile. We had no washing facilities and every morning he would roll up his shirt sleeves and tuck the top of his shirt in and have a thorough wash in a small enamel bowl which he stood on the side cupboard. Having no tap except in the outside yard we all used the same water afterwards. Heaven knows whether we were clean, but we felt clean.

My mother was born in Neal Street, Covent Garden. Her father came from Ireland and his family were Roman Catholic. Her father worked as a porter in Covent Garden Market and we were told as children that he could carry more baskets on his head than anyone else. My grandmother came from Maidstone and Alice, my eldest sister, said that she saw her once when we went hop picking in Kent. I think that she must have come to London to work as a maid. My mother had a very dependable older sister who died in the influenza epidemic in 1918. My sister Alice maintained that had she lived, our home would have been quite different.

As a young woman my mother had long hair and I remember on one occasion being allowed to comb it. She was small in stature but although her arms and legs were very thin, she was immensely strong and wiry. I remember her strength when she was chopping wood by the fire. She had a very long face for her size and big bulbous eyes and a long nose. I don't remember her ever laughing but then she had little to laugh about. As a child I was never happy about the way she looked. Her clothes, like ours, were always cast offs from other people. She used to pull up her lisle stockings as far as her knees and sort of twist them round above the knee and tuck in the rest. I can't imagine how they ever kept up!

I believe that she loved my father in an undemonstrative way. I can't remember her ever once fondling or kissing us. She was fondest of Alice in a rather deferential way. When Alice started working it made all the difference to our lives. She sometimes brought home food for us when she got her wages. My mother provided a hot mid-day meal and sometimes a roly-poly pudding or stewed fruit and custard. Sunday dinner was always a sausage and mash. At tea there was a piece of bread and dripping and then nothing else that day. My father was sometimes given a boiled egg and then we all stood round with a slither of bread and one by one dipped it into the yolk. Although eggs were bigger in those days, there can hardly have been much left for him.

My mother, to clear her head, would take a pinch of snuff! We had no handkerchiefs and only torn off bits of rag for our monthly periods. I used to watch her enjoy her jug of ale and on winter nights she would heat the poker until it was red hot and then hold it in the ale.

When we had earache she would tie a sweaty sock of my father's around our face and funnily enough it seemed to cure it. She never appeared to have any friends although she would sometimes chat on the stairs to the woman who lived above. I remember so well the picture of her coming along Great Titchfield Street carrying a large galvanised bath filled with wet washing which she had carried all the way from Marshall Street Baths. I used to think "How strong she is!" But now I think, "How tired she must have been!" The adjective put in the Church worker's book to describe my mother was 'Unsatisfactory!' She was just improvident and unable to make life better for us or herself. She was not a good enough manager to be poor! I feel differently looking back now as an adult and have much more understanding. It was only when I left home that I began to see my father and mother as real people and feel for their difficulties.

My mother had seven of us but she lost one and so there were six of us to look after. I saw other families fare much better than we did. I never quite knew how much my father gave for the housekeeping. He used to put sometimes half a crown on the mantelpiece towards our rent. The rent for these miserable rooms was eight shilling and fourpence a week. That was a lot of money in those days. Henry Holmes was our landlord and he had an office in Mortimer Street. There were often loud rows and quarrels that took place between my mother and father; these were nearly all to do with money. My father would leave the rent and then later find out that it hadn't been paid by my mother. My father was very upright and honest. My eldest sister Alice inherited a lot of my father's honesty. Always during the quarrels my father would say: "This all started with you moving into these kitchens"

My feelings at the time were all with my father. As a young child I was so often ashamed of my mother who never took any care of herself except perhaps sometimes on a Sunday evening when she would smarten up a little and my father would say to us: "We are going for a stroll uptown." That meant for a walk along Regent Street to look at the shops and calling in for a drink on the way back. We were always given a halfpenny each to spend on these occasions.

Sometimes I was called upon to do unpleasant jobs for my mother, such as going up the stairs and telling the Tally Man (who had come for his weekly shilling to pay off money lent previously) that my mother wasn't in. I was always nervous that he might push me aside and come down stairs. There was a bell hanging on a chain which rang and then as our top door was always open he would be able to come in and come down the stairs. I'm sure that in the long run my mother had to pay back very much more than the £1 which she had originally borrowed. Another very disagreeable task was being sent to the pawn shop. My mother would sometimes pawn the people's laundry that she had taken in to mangle. I used to be terrified that customers would come back for their washing before I had got it back from the pawn broker. The pawnbroker was quite a walk away and all would seem well to me until I had to enter the shop, give the pawn ticket and the money, redeem the washing, and then get back home trying not to be seen. I hated meeting any of my friends on the way home but sometimes the bundle of washing would be quite big and just could not be disguised. One day my elder brother managed to buy himself a decent pair of trousers for Sunday wear; you can imagine his fury when my mother pawned them. On many occasions I've been sent to the pawn shop and told to hurry in case my brother arrived back early. My brother had quite a temper. If we younger ones made too much noise he would shout at us. My brother was not out of place in any society. He always looked smart. He grew to be tall and handsome and was very intelligent. He was also musical and learnt so much classical music listening through earphones to lunch-hour concerts on the radio.

Another man I dreaded was the rent man; this was because we were generally in arrears. I was also worried lest he would turn us out onto the street with nowhere to go. I knew that a home was a home however poor.

I can never remember my parents coming anywhere with us for an outing except on one occasion when my father took my brother Ted and me for a long walk over Westminster Bridge. It just wasn't the custom at all. Children played in the street learning to socialise with all age groups without adult interference. Children were quite safe in the streets playing together. The older children of the family took charge of the younger ones. All children took themselves to school without adult supervision.

Sunday School and School

I was a terrible baby, always crying so I was told. They said that any one just had to look at me and I cried! Because of this I was called 'water melon'. I can remember hiding behind my mother's skirts. When I started school I told myself that I must try to stop crying so much. This I did. I must have been about perhaps three years old when I was taken by my sister Alice to Sunday school. The infants met in Buckingham Street and Miss Frere took the very tiny children. She came from a famous missionary family and so it was in her blood to spread the Christian Gospel. The first genuine love I felt in my life came from her. She wore a long full skirt and a straw hat tied with a scarf under her chin. She would sit on a little stool and hold out her arms to us as we were led in. She taught us all delightful little songs for small children that I still remember well:

> Jesus loves me this I know
> For the Bible tells me so.
> Little ones to him belong
> We are weak but He is strong.

And another one that gave me much pleasure because it told me that I was loved:

Yes Jesus loves me, yes Jesus loves me,
Yes Jesus loves me, the Bible tells me so.

We little ones were taken for a yearly treat to Kew Gardens. I can still see the brake pulled by the four large horses. It was open on both sides with slatted seats for the little ones to sit on. I can't remember getting to Kew Gardens but I can remember the great excitement of that journey. I can still feel that excitement as our older brothers and sisters waved us off.

Then came real school and I loved every minute at my school. At first my elder sister took me, but I soon managed to go there on my own, and I always got there very early. At the age of seven I was moved up to a junior school. One incident I recall which teachers may not do today: the teacher took me on her knee after school to teach me how to make French knots. It is still vivid to me. It was with bright yellow thread and I managed to do a whole row. She gave me a little silver threepenny bit for learning so quickly.

To me school represented a bright, clean and well-ordered environment. I loved it as it was so very different from the disorder and lack of beauty at home. The décor was excellent with interesting and beautiful pictures. Gradually my shyness slipped away and I was able to shine at verse speaking. When I look back I consider myself so very fortunate in having a teacher so keen on poetry; this influence on me has lasted for the whole of my life and I still give lectures on the Romantic poets and their poetry.

Every morning we would all gather in the main hall for prayers. Miss Cox, the headmistress sometimes took the prayers from the General Thanksgiving and left out the words Jesus Christ because children of other faiths were present. Miss Goff was young, enthusiastic and very modern. She had short bobbed hair and much shorter skirts than the other teachers. She gave me my love of poetry. Later she was whisked off to Burlington High School. In my time children moved up each year but kept the same teacher. However, after Miss Goff left I was lucky to come under Miss Head. I only hope that one day in eternity we shall meet so that I may thank her for all that she gave me during my formative years. She was fairly tall and well built, but not too overweight. She used to wear light voile dresses in different colours, sometimes blue, sometimes green and sometimes yellow. She had a full face with a fairly pale skin and greeny-blue eyes. I always admired her hair. This was a crown of glory - very fair and long but always worn in a bun and little wisps of curly hair would stray away.

In the break two teachers would be with us in the playground, and they would walk up and down with their teacups, talking animatedly together. I would often follow them at a safe distance. Then the whistle would go and we would form lines into our respective classes and would be led back into the school. Other teachers would take us for history or for singing. Miss Head was the geography and poetry teacher. She was so enthusiastic herself and keen for us to learn. With her enthusiasm and guidance I learnt so very many wonderful poems from a wide range of poets. We learnt so many poems by heart and now although I am in my eighties I still can recite many of them completely. 'The Walrus and the Carpenter', 'How They Brought the Good News from Ghent to Aix', 'Ulysses' and many poems by Wordsworth. All these poems have become my friends and I feel that even if I lost my immediate memory they would still be there and obtainable.

I was entered for the North London Poetry Festival each year and so was often given extra tuition. Once I remember, the chosen poem was 'O Captain My Captain' by W E Henley and when I arrived there with my teacher I found that the majority of those attending were boys who gave excellent renderings. As I was exceedingly small for my age it must have been quite amusing to see me mount the large stage and give my interpretation. On this occasion, I remember, I got Highly Commended. When I won my Poetry Society Medal I was so worried as I had to ask my father for two shillings and sixpence to pay for the medal that I had won. I remember hopping from foot to foot after receiving the usual half penny. My father looked up and said, "Well shouldn't you be off now or you'll be late for school."
"Please Dad can I have two and six?"
"What on earth for! Do you think I'm made of money?"
In the end he counted out the money with his stained fingers and I was able to receive my medal.

People have often asked me how it is that I have not got a cockney accent. This poetry recitation helped me, but my brothers and sisters also had good voices. I was hopeless at Maths and though I could recite the tables well, I never did understand how they could be used. I was always very good, though, at anything physical, such as running, jumping and netball. I never felt happy, though, about our lack of money because I couldn't ever join in when the children brought money for special things at school. After the First World War anyone who had money to spare would buy War Loan certificates. Children would come to school with the appropriate money to buy a stamp for these. I could never imagine myself ever having the money to be able to purchase one.

As I was living in a highly populated Jewish community a good half of the school were Jewish. At playtime a Jewish mother would come to the gate of the school and hand her child a bagel filled with cream cheese. I would hang around and sometimes when the parent had left I would be given the delicious bagel. It was a real red letter day when this happened. The taste of this treat has never been excelled for me. I always experienced great fascination for the Jewish children. They were generally highly talented and walked off with the scholarships to higher schools. They were all so very different. Some had very dark hair and eyes, others were fair and all seemed beautiful except for a girl called Millie; she was about twice my size in height and girth. Even my beloved teacher, Miss Head, came in for criticism in my thoughts because Millie was very short sighted and wore thick glasses. One day when she presented her work, Miss Head refused to mark it as it was so messy, full of blots and the end of the pages were crumpled. She took hold of the book by a corner of a page and threw it across the table. I was perhaps too sensitive and shed tears for Millie.

Birth, Health and Death

When my youngest sister was going to be born I was sent round to Mrs Church who lived behind us in the better half of Charlton Street. Her fee was two shillings and sixpence. I believe she delivered most of the babies in the area. She was rather robust, clean-looking with a down-to-earth manner. She came immediately and got us to get her plenty of hot water and as many newspapers as possible. She then sent us out of the way and we went out to play. I remember asking my father where babies came from and he said that they came out of his bag. Some time later I learnt the truth from friends.

Joan slept in the same big bed as my mother and father and then when she got older she slept at the bottom of the bed. One day I felt that some change was needed to be made so I asked my father if he could get a little truckle bed for Joan to come and be in our room. I remember the excitement when Joan came to sleep with all of us. Alice slept in the big bed between Marge and me and I can remember the wonderful warmth of our arms around each other; when one turned we all had to turn. This kept us cosy on a cold night. We often had to put all our coats on the bed to keep us warm on winter nights. We were so glad of the chamber pot under the bed which was used by us every night.

Before I was ten I was not ill very often. However I remember before this age I stood watching a large pot of potatoes boiling on the gas stove. I was singing and tapping the handle in time to my song when suddenly it tipped over and the boiling water went all over my foot. I was in agony and a great blister soon covered my foot. When my father came home he took one look and said that I must go to the hospital. I was wheeled in a pram and when the doctor saw it he burst the blister and all the liquid came out. It took some time to heal afterwards. I almost always had sore knees and elbows because I ran everywhere, jumping over gratings and leaping in the air and inevitably falling over. I still have childhood scars on my elbows and knees to this day. We are often told that our bodies are constantly being renewed, however I still have these scars. I remember the temptation to pick at the scabs when they were nearly healed underneath.

When I was quite young I started getting a series of sties on my eyes. I had a record number of five on one eye. Alice complained bitterly when she had to take me to the clinic to have them bathed because it made her late for work. When I cried she said: 'You haven't anything like the pain when I bit my tongue almost in two. Our Aunt Alice took me to the cupboard and poured salt into the wound and rushed me to hospital.' I must admit, thinking about it now, that the pain of the salt in the wound must have been indescribable. Poor Alice hated having to go in late to work because of me. One time, to her great humiliation, she had to take me to have my hair cleansed. I used to dread the nurse who came into school to inspect all our heads. She would sit on a stool and have a bowl of disinfectant and a very long steel comb. We were ushered in one by one to her office. She was not at all gentle and would take hold of my hair in a rough way. She would examine it several times to look for nits and all their eggs. Sometimes I managed to get away without her noticing. Later my sister started a combing session with us younger ones. She would get a piece of newspaper and a tooth comb and clean our hair and skulls. This effort had to be constantly repeated and because she did this it kept us away from the cleansing station. I can remember sitting down and having a cap put on. What this cap contained I do not know, but after some time with it on the hair was then washed. Everyone in my class knew about this cap because of the smell.

When I was about 10 years old my legs became very, very painful – so painful that I couldn't walk. The clinic doctor said at the time that I was suffering from rheumatism and I was sent away with another girl from the parish called Miriam who was very poor like me to a convalescent home in Broadstairs for three months. Here I began walking again. What a tremendous life-giving organisation this was. I think that it was run by the Church. Nothing like it seems to exist today; at that time there were many convalescent homes where people went after severe illness. For me it was heaven on earth. We went for the winter months leading up to Christmas. I was put at a table where I was expected to eat twice as much as the others as I was so very much underweight. We were weighed every week. I only put on three pounds though during the long stay. The meals were very special; on Mondays we were given a very thick soup with every kind of bean in it. I have never been able to reproduce the taste of that delicious Broadstairs soup. On Sundays I was not so keen on the meal as it was a cold one: beetroot, potatoes and sliced meat followed by ice-cream. Every afternoon we were put outside to sleep with a blanket over us. We all came from poor backgrounds.

Just as Christmas came we were given a wonderful party and each one of us was presented with a gift from Father Christmas who was the local Parson. Just at the end of the presentation, very suddenly, his hair and his beard caught fire from one of the lighted candles on the tree. I believe his long beard caught fire first. Suddenly his whole being seemed to be ablaze. He broke through a glass door and rolled himself over and over in the snow. Luckily this put out the flames. We children dropped our presents and ran crying from the room. I remember I had been given a black china doll. Luckily it had not broken. Much later we were all taken in to see Father Christmas, now all bandaged but still able to smile at us.

Every day we were taken for a walk along the seashore and after one stormy night I remember seeing starfish flattened and stuck to the sea wall. I enjoyed every day so very much. It was a very sad time when we all had to return to London. I wept bitterly in the bus taking us to the station. By the time we reached the station every child was crying. When finally I reached home I went into the lavatory in the backyard and sat on the seat sobbing; it seemed such a terrible change of scenery and life.

My sister Margaret was also sent to a convalescent home as she was suffering from an illness called Saint Vitus Dance. She used to kick us under the table and always seemed to keep moving, being unable to stay still. My mother took her on a very lovely summer day to the convalescent home in Brighton, leaving the baby with me and Eve. The day wore on and it grew quite late and the baby had been crying for a long time as she needed feeding. She did not have a bottle as my Mother fed her. So Eve and I went to the police station in Tottenham Court Road and saw a police officer. He bent down over the counter and asked us very politely what we wanted. I told him that my mother had not come back home and that the baby needed feeding. His reply was: "Now you get back home and before long your mother will be home." We hurried back and sure enough to my great relief my mother was there, sitting feeding Joan. I wondered how the police officer knew. I asked my mother why she was so late. Her reply was that she sat on the pebbles in the sunshine and was so enjoying herself that she forgot the time and the baby.

Children often died of severe illness because there were no antibiotics. There were separate hospitals for infectious illnesses such as scarlet fever and diphtheria. Whenever Eve and I saw an ambulance coming towards us we would catch hold of our collars and say very quickly as it passed:

Touch collar, never swallow, Never get the fever,
Not for you, not for me,
Not for all the family.

Once I was very ill with a quinsy. That was one of the very few times that I saw my mother crying. We were in an ambulance taking me to a hospital. She told me that she was crying because they were sending me to the hospital where most people never came out! The other time I saw her cry was when her brother died. We didn't know that she had a brother and she had never mentioned him before.

My mother sometimes drank too much and I always knew when she had had too much to drink because she would fold her arms and sit in a strange position, her voice would be slurred and her face flushed. Once when she was like this and my father had also drunk too much, my mother and father had a quarrel and then he said that he was going out. I knew that he was not in a fit state to go out, so I threw his bowler hat away right to the end of the dark passage. I knew that he would never go out without his hat. I was so relieved when I saw him take off his trousers and get into bed. In the morning nothing was said.

Many people used to frequent the pub called The Ship. It was around the corner from us in Upper Marylebone Street. The Ship is still there but the street has been renamed. People would often say, 'We go to the pub to drown our sorrows.' I could never understand this as it appeared to me that it caused a lot of trouble and unhappiness. Little children used to sit on the ground waiting for their parents to come home, often in the very cold. Sometimes a very large biscuit would be obtained in the pub and often you would see children pacified with this. I also tasted one once and remember finding it very satisfying.

The publicans received a large amount from the wages of the poor that should of course have been spent on food and maintaining the families. Friday night and Saturday night were the worst nights for heavy drinking. By Sunday most of the money was spent and so it was generally a much quieter day. There was usually a Bobby on the street and he would deal with any disturbances. This was usually done by himself but if he needed help he would blow his police whistle which would immediately summon help from another policeman or from people nearby.

People were always paid in cash and none of these people ever went into a bank. Any money they had left would be stored under the mattress. Many earned just eight shillings or ten shillings a week. There were no children's allowances or social service payments to make up low wages nor was there such a thing as a minimum wage and so people were often hungry. There were no contraceptives and new pregnancies were often immediately aborted with a large dose of castor oil. My mother had a child every three years so she must have had her own way of dealing with this problem. Deaths of adults were frequent and many children died before they were very old.

Funerals were very solemn and ritualistic affairs. Everyone from the oldest to the very youngest relative wore black. The body of the deceased would remain in the coffin in the front room and the relatives and neighbours would all come in to pay their respects. If money was available there was a great show when the carriage carrying the hearse would be drawn by two horses; each grand horse was covered with a great black pall and the glass-sided hearse would be decorated with flowers. There was a great deal of gossip as to the qualities and way of life of the dead relation or neighbour.

Jewish funerals were quite different. They sat by the dead person for three days, taking it in turns to be there so the dead were never left alone. Then for the funeral they would engage professional paid mourners, so Eve and I would follow behind the long line of family mourners and be paid to join in the wailing. This wailing went on while the whole procession walked round the nearest block of about ten houses seven times. We were young but we were very good wailers and enjoyed this. Black was worn for about three months following the death of a close relative and after that for the rest of the year a wide black band would be worn on the arm of a coat.

When Eve was about five years old she caught diphtheria and almost died. I remember seeing her sitting up in a huge family bed looking very small and very pale. Her younger brother and baby sister died of diphtheria and this was a great blow to the family. Eve's mother wore herself out caring for them. Eve's father had an open wound in his stomach from the First World War. It was permanently bandaged, but when he drank too much the wound would cause trouble. Eve was afraid of her father who was very severe if they were late home or messed up their shoes. He had a job as a delivery driver for Waring and Gillows which was a very caring firm, looking after their employees.

It was not an uncommon sight to see very disfigured and crippled people. At this stage there were many deaths from septicaemia following surgery. There were many dwarves and midgets. Old people's skin was very crinkled and wrinkled and was the colour of parchment. A great number were elderly widows who came to the big houses in the area to work as servants and housemaids. Many lived in one room in large tenement houses, living I don't know how on practically nothing. Their diet mainly consisted of tea and bread and a little extra supplied by the church or a charity. I sometimes went to the Mother's Union to entertain some of these people. A Miss Alnut ran the meeting and she tried to get an interesting speaker each week. In the winter there would be a huge fire with a great guard round it and the warmth would send them off to sleep. Miss Alnut would clap her hands and say, 'Come on, Ladies, you must keep awake for the speaker wants to tell you about his missionary work.' They would open their eyes for a very brief spell and then off they would go again until they heard the tea cups rattle. They really came for the warmth and the tea. If anyone was absent she would go round to see if they needed help. I believe that the great work of these dedicated helpers is written in the scrolls of Heaven.

A LIBERAL AND GODLY DEAN

INDEX